W9-ARY-785

HOW TO USE THIS BOOK

By air you can cross the Rockies in forty-five minutes. By car it takes less than a day. But to discover the region's Anasazi Indian heritage and the story of its mining aristocracy, to fish its best streams and hike the land that was the main line west for those bound for the promised land, to see the work of its best artists, past and present, and more wildlife than you're likely to find anywhere else in America, it takes a little longer.

Welcome to the completely updated 1993 edition *2 to 22 Days in the Rockies*, the self-guiding itinerary planner that shows you why these mountains are a favorite playground not only of Americans but also of international travelers who return again and again. This guide doesn't merely inventory some of the region's greatest assets, it shows you step by step how to find your way to the very best of Colorado, Wyoming, Montana, and Idaho. Along the way you will cross the Continental Divide at least four times, float some of the best rivers, fish the finest streams, and explore historic cliff dwellings. You'll enjoy a secluded dude ranch at a modest price, drive up a 14,000-foot mountain, take a horseback, mountain bike, or jeep trip into the wilderness, and see where marble was quarried for the Lincoln Memorial. You'll also see some of America's finest mountain scenery, a region famous for its snow-capped peaks, waterfalls, wildflowers, and uncrowded trails. And this year, you'll be able to join the special 150th anniversary celebration of the Oregon Trail.

The modular 22-day format is a loop trip beginning in Denver, crossing the Colorado Rockies to Mesa Verde, heading north through Dinosaur National Park, the Grand Tetons, and Yellowstone before heading back through historic South Pass and the Medicine Bow National Forest to Rocky Mountain National Park, Boulder, and Denver. For readers with more time, an itinerary extension makes it possible to see highlights of the Colorado Springs/Pikes Peak/Cripple Creek, Colorado,

region. There is also extensive information on traveling to
Montana and Idaho highlights such as Glacier National
Park, the Sawtooth National Recreation Area, Sun Valley,
and Craters of the Moon National Monument. If you have
less than 22 days, by all means pick up the itinerary at any
point along the route and enjoy as much as you can. You
can take the balance of the trip at a later date.

As the author or coauthor of three previous 22 Days
books—California, Asia, and Around the World—I've
personally field-tested every mile of this route. My
choices, based on more than 20 years' experience visiting
every part of the Rockies, encompass both perennial
favorites such as Glenwood Springs and Old Faithful and
lesser-known treasures like Flaming Gorge and Redstone.
While every traveler has a different style, we all want to
enjoy a relaxing, hassle-free trip that takes in the best a
region has to offer. That's why the 2 to 22 Days series
authors, myself included, actually visit all the sites
described in our books, sleep in the motels, inns, or
campgrounds, and eat at the restaurants we recommend.
All our endorsements come from the heart. We travel
anonymously, pay our own bills, and accept no subsidies
from any of the recommended establishments. The result
is the kind of tour plan you would recommend to your
best friend or relative.

As you orient yourself to this region, you'll discover
that simply traversing the 200-mile-wide Rockies region
from east to west isn't good enough. Transcontinental
travelers usually settle for just a narrow slice of this
famous area. By going north and south as well as east and
west, you can follow the Rockies for more than 1,000
miles from New Mexico to the Canadian border and
beyond. Our chosen route shows you how to see the best
of this region in a practical manner. Although the book is
organized around a loop beginning and ending in Denver, the trip can easily begin at other points. For example,
travelers coming from northern California may want to
begin and end their trip at Dinosaur National Monument
in Utah, the westernmost point of the trip (see Itinerary
section for more details). If you're coming from Arizona,

2 to 22 DAYS IN THE ROCKIES

THE ITINERARY PLANNER

1993 Edition

ROGER RAPOPORT

John Muir Publications
Santa Fe, New Mexico

ACKNOWLEDGMENTS

My wife, Margot, and our children, Jonathan and Elizabeth, all helped in the quest for the perfect three-star attraction. I also want to thank George Lind, Anne Olivas, Carl Olivas, Anna and Larry Shugart, Liz Lind, Carlene Lind, Peter Beren, Bill Martin, Pam Hodel, Linda Sauer, Carla Hunt, Georgia Smith, and the chambers of commerce and tourist boards of the five states and many local areas covered in these pages. A special thanks to my friends in Santa Fe at John Muir Publications.

In memory of George Lind, who knew and loved the Rockies

Other JMP travel guidebooks by the author
Great Cities of Eastern Europe
2 to 22 Days in California
2 to 22 Days in Asia (with Burl Willes)
22 Days Around the World (with Burl Willes)

John Muir Publications, P.O. Box 613, Santa Fe, NM 87504

1993 edition

ISSN 1058-6083
ISBN 1-56261-081-3

Distributed to the book trade by:
W. W. Norton & Company, Inc.
New York, New York

Design Mary Shapiro
Maps Holly Wood
Cover photo Leo de Wys, Inc./Everett C. Johnson
Typography Copygraphics, Inc.
Printer McNaughton & Gunn, Inc.

CONTENTS

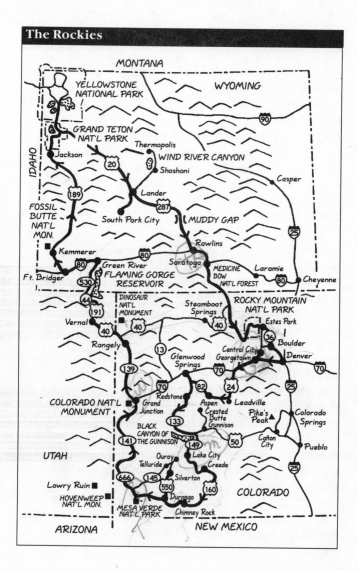

The Rockies

MONTANA

WYOMING

YELLOWSTONE NATIONAL PARK

90

GRAND TETON NAT'L PARK

Thermopolis

WIND RIVER CANYON

Jackson

IDAHO

20

Shoshoni

Casper

189

Lander

287

FOSSIL BUTTE NAT'L MON.

South Park City

MUDDY GAP

25

Kemmerer

Rawlins

80

80

Green River

Saratoga

Laramie

FLAMING GORGE RESERVOIR

MEDICINE BOW NAT'L FOREST

Ft. Bridger

530

80

Cheyenne

44

DINOSAUR NAT'L MONUMENT

Steamboat Springs

ROCKY MOUNTAIN NAT'L PARK

191

Vernal

40

40

Estes Park

36

Boulder

Rangely

13

Glenwood Springs

Central City Georgetown

Denver

139

70

70

82

24

25

COLORADO NAT'L MONUMENT

70

Redstone

Aspen

Leadville

Pike's Peak

Colorado Springs

Grand Junction

Crested Butte Gunnison

133

BLACK CANYON OF THE GUNNISON

141

149

50

Cañon City

Pueblo

UTAH

Lake City

Ouray

Telluride

Creede

25

Lowry Ruin

666

145

Silverton

550

160

COLORADO

HOVENWEEP NAT'L MON.

Durango

MESA VERDE NAT'L PARK

Chimney Rock

ARIZONA

NEW MEXICO

you may want to start in the Durango area. And travelers from the Northwest or western Canada may find it easiest to begin at Yellowstone National Park. This itinerary is structured so that you'll be able to drive in a leisurely manner with plenty of time out to enjoy the region's best trails, ghost towns, rodeos, and hot springs. While the route is flexible, a basic trip plan helps keep you focused on having a good time instead of worrying about mundane details and sorting through dozens of brochures. The book tells you where to go and how to get there, offers lodging suggestions in all price categories, and recommends reliable restaurants, outfitters, and attractions. Like a compass, it will keep you on track.

This book comes with numerous itinerary options and extensions. Each one gives you the opportunity to augment the basic 22-day itinerary as your time and interests allow. As you begin planning your trip, feel free to adjust this plan to meet your needs. (More on that subject in a minute.) But first let's take a look at the itinerary format, divided into 22 daily sections containing:

1. A **suggested schedule** for each day's travel and sightseeing. Follow it hour by hour, or, if you wish, modify it to suit your convenience.

2. A detailed **travel route** description for each driving segment of your trip.

3. **Descriptive overviews** and **sightseeing highlights** (rated in order of importance for the day in question: ▲▲▲ Don't miss; ▲▲ Try hard to see; and ▲ See if you get a chance).

4. Suggested **restaurants** as well as **lodging or campground** for each night of the trip.

5. **Practical tips**—random tidbits that will help make your trip go well.

6. **Itinerary options**—excursion suggestions for travelers who have extra time.

7. User-friendly **maps** designed to show you what the road up ahead is really like.

Why Take the 2- to 22-Day Approach?
Professional tour operators spend a great deal of time
designing guided trips to a number of the areas covered
in this book. Many travelers who go on their own take a
serendipitous approach, stopping at the name attractions
and anything else that strikes their fancy. Either method
can work if you like being led around or are prepared to
travel in hit-or-miss fashion. But if you've ever been
stuck at a boring luncheon, had a tour guide herd you
away from a wonderful landmark before you were ready
to leave, reached a famous museum on the day it was
closed, or had a big fight with your spouse or best friend
over directions, you know some of the pitfalls to these
approaches. Many readers turn to thick guidebooks
chock-full of lengthy lists of attractions. Many are excellent, particularly if you live in the city in question or are
planning an extended stay. But it can be slow going when
the chapters don't parallel your route or you are hungry
and have to wade through a list of 70 restaurants to find
what you have in mind. In addition, it is unfortunately
the case that even name guides may include material written by authors who have never visited some of the areas
in question or haven't revisited them for years.

No matter how long you have to spend in the Rockies,
all these problems are conveniently solved by the 22-day
approach. First, you're the boss, in effect your own guide,
working with the same kind of itinerary the classy tour
companies use. My recommendations are a consensus
choice based not only on the views of the experts and
lifelong residents of the Rockies but also on the opinions
of numerous visitors I've debriefed while researching this
book and local tourism experts who've explored this area
all their lives. As we researched this route together, my
wife and children contributed their assessments in an
effort to make this trip as exciting for kids as it is for
adults. The result is a practical trip plan for a region that
offers more thrills per mile than just about any other
place I can think of. If you think I'm exaggerating, please
take a minute to consider the evidence. Part of the fun of
writing this book was revisiting some of my favorite

Rockies haunts such as Leadville and Durango. Nearly all these destinations seem to have improved over time with better hotels and restaurants, more museums, and back-country attractions. Once you leave Denver, you'll dis-cover the region's rural splendor. And even the most popular national parks, such as the Grand Tetons, offer seemingly endless wilderness opportunities. As you make your way through the region, keep in mind that the 2 to 22 Days plan is not necessarily one you have to enjoy in a single trip. If your time is limited, say, only a week, con-sider following the first-, second-, or third-week itiner-ary to see one part of the region such as the Wyoming national parks. If you are on a business trip to Denver and only have a free weekend, by all means focus on that por-tion of the book and save the rest for a return visit. Because there is good air service to major Rockies desti-nations such as Aspen, Durango, Grand Junction, Colorado Springs, Jackson Hole, Kalispell, Missoula, and the Sun Valley area, you can easily jump between regions to sample different parts of the states. Feel free to adjust or augment the suggested itinerary as you see fit. And don't be discouraged if you can't see it all. Getting back to the Rockies only takes a few hours by air.

If you've already signed up for a tour or are traveling with a group, you'll also find this book useful. Every tour builds in a considerable amount of free time, even free days. Some give you several free pre- or posttour days. Use these opportunities to pursue some of the sugges-tions in this book. Or, if you prefer, break off from sched-uled events, luncheons, shopping tours, or other low pri-ority events to follow some of our suggestions. It's not uncommon for experienced travelers to leave a tour for a day or two in order to pursue other possibilities on their own.

One of the most gratifying aspects of writing 2 to 22 Days books is receiving letters from satisfied readers who appreciate the many advantages of self-guided itinerary planning. Not sidetracked by tourist traps, they have the time to make great finds, often only a few minutes away from the overrated and overpriced. Because the itinerary is flexible—you can change the schedule anytime you feel like it—there's no problem stopping along the way to hole up at a classy resort, dude ranch, or campground by a stream. Take as much time as you want and then resume the itinerary. In other words, you can slow down whenever you feel like it, a far cry from the forced march that characterizes too many guided tours today. By taking a balanced approach, you'll return home well rested and ready to go to work to pay for your next vacation.

How Much Will It Cost?

How much do you want to spend? We know people who do this itinerary on a bare bones budget, camping every night, never eating out, and skipping nightlife. Budget travelers can figure on spending about $45 to $65 a night on a motel room for two. A moderate room will run an average of $65 to $90 a night. If you're looking for deluxe accommodations, expect to pay about $100 to $200 a night. Bed and breakfasts average $60 to $90 a night, slightly less for home stays. Hostels charge about $12 per night. You can camp in public parks for $8 to $15 a night, while private campgrounds run about $15 to $30. Naturally, prices in rural areas run less than the big cities, and you can get some excellent bargains in the spring and fall. You may also find special summer packages in the popular winter resort areas.

If you're driving in your own car, base your gas estimates on approximately 2,600 miles within Colorado, Utah, and Wyoming. The extension to Montana and Idaho adds another 1,450 miles. For the Colorado Springs region extension, add about 300 miles. Of course, you'll also want to add in mileage from your home to the point where you begin the 22-day loop. Keep in mind that most of this route is not on interstates and that there are some stretches of mountain driving that you will want to enjoy at reduced speeds. On balance, you can expect to average about 45 miles per hour, which, incidentally, happens to be the speed limit in the national parks.

Looking at the map, you'll probably wonder why I've chosen one route over another. Unless you're a trucker barreling across the Rockies with no interest in the sights, this region is, with a few notable exceptions, best seen from two-lane blacktop. All the routes I've chosen are safe and well engineered, but I don't always use the most direct route from point A to B. This itinerary has been shaped to lead you through the very best of the Rockies, deliberately dodging the dull and predictable. You'll also be delighted to know that on long stretches traffic will be extremely light, a definite plus on a trip of this kind. One of the great contributions of the interstate highway system is the way it has sucked virtually all of the truck traffic and most of the motorists off older scenic routes chosen for this itinerary. As a result, you'll be king of the road.

To calculate food costs, figure inexpensive restaurant meals at under $12 for dinner, moderate establishments at $12 to $25, and expensive choices at over $25. Budget about $5 to $8 per person per meal for breakfast and lunch. If you are doing your own cooking or picnicking for lunch (as I do), these meals will cost about the same as they do at home.

Admission to state and national parks averages $5. Most of the museums on the tour are under $5, and many are free. Figure a total of about $175 per person for recommended tours and museums in this book. Figure $30 for a short raft trip, $50 for a half-day excursion, and $80 to $100 for an all-day trip. Naturally, you'll want to add in the price of any special interest tours, bike rentals, or horseback tours.

When to Go

This itinerary is designed for the May to October period. Spring and fall are delightful in this region. If the weather is cooperative, these are ideal times to beat the crowds. Unfortunately, sudden snowstorms can descend on this region as late as June and as early as September. When you add in the fact that many national park facilities and resorts begin shutting down shortly after Labor Day, it's clear that summer is the optimum time for a visit. Because winter is peak season for a number of resort

areas covered in this book, you'll generally find that
towns like Aspen and Durango have plenty of room in the
summer. There's also good availability in Denver. This is
not the case in the national parks and Jackson Hole, Wyoming, where advance reservations are mandatory for
resorts, hotels, and motels. They are also a good idea for
those who are traveling by RV or camping.

If you decide to visit in late spring or early fall, be sure
to bring along some cold weather gear, such as a winter
jacket, hat, and gloves, just in case there is a sudden
storm. Even summer visitors are advised to carry a warm
jacket, sweater, and, of course, rain gear. You may find it
necessary to adapt this itinerary in the event of a sudden
snowstorm. But passes typically are closed only for a
short period by these freak events.

Numerous art and music festivals as well as other special events will add to your enjoyment of a Rockies trip.
You may even want to plan your trip dates around special
performances at the Central City Opera, Aspen Music Festival, or the Jackson Hole summer concert series. To
avoid disappointments along your route, remember to
double-check for holiday closings at museums.

Transportation

Many airlines provide nonstop service to Denver from all
major American cities. It's also easy to fly to cities like
Aspen, Durango, and Jackson Hole if you prefer to begin
your trip in one of these communities. Amtrak's *California Zephyr* stops in Denver, Granby (Rocky Mountain
National Park), and Glenwood Springs. *The Pioneer*
serves Idaho points, including Shoshone near Sun Valley.
There are also bus connections to many of the cities on
this route. If you don't drive to the Rockies, you'll want to
rent a car when you reach Denver. Although there are a
few stretches of unpaved road, you won't need a four-
wheel-drive vehicle. Drivers of large RVs may find the route
from Leadville to Aspen over Independence Pass too narrow
for their liking. They may prefer to take Interstate 70 west
to Glenwood Springs and head south to Aspen from
there. In addition, if you're taking the Montana itinerary

option, keep in mind that the Going to the Sun Highway does not allow vehicles over 30 feet in length between July 1 and August 31. The rest of the season, the maximum size is 35 feet long and 8 feet wide. If you have extended mirrors on your vehicle, fold or remove them when you are not towing.

Before leaving home, you'll want to check out your vehicle to make sure that it can handle steep mountain grades, hot- and cold-weather driving, and back roads. Although you'll never be more than 50 miles from emergency road service, you can avoid downtime by carrying a basic auto tool kit and repair manual, spare V-belts, radiator hoses, a good spare tire, and extra radiator coolant. Should you plan on renting an RV in Denver, consider choosing a mini motor home; you'll appreciate their maneuverability and relatively decent gas mileage; large motor homes are recommended only for groups of more than four. A number of national chains, such as Cruise America (800-327-7778) or Budget (800-222-6772), rent RVs in the Denver area. The Denver Convention and Visitors Bureau at 225 W. Colfax, Denver, CO 80202 (303-892-1112) can suggest additional RV rental companies.

Food and Lodging
This is one of the stickiest areas for all travelers to unfamiliar areas. To simplify your trip, I've suggested many restaurants in all price categories. In addition to well-known establishments, a sampling of newer dining spots serving popular regional and ethnic cuisine is included; you'll have a chance to enjoy prime rib, fresh trout, locally smoked pork chops, vegetarian dishes, fajitas, pasta dishes, barbecue, salad bars, and haute cuisine. If you're the kind of traveler who likes to search out spots popular with the local community or who enjoys a dining room with a panoramic view, I have some promising suggestions. Naturally, I also suggest picnic spots for lunch. Not only is this a good way to save money but it's also a pleasant way to visit some of a state's fine parks. A lightweight cooler stocked from a local deli is a must for any serious traveler in the Rockies.

If you're planning to stay in hotels, you'll find it's easier to get reservations in rural areas during the week. Reservations are mandatory in the national park lodges, some resorts, dude ranches, and Jackson, Wyoming. If you're traveling during a holiday period, reservations are a must everywhere. In general, availability in the cities is much better on weekends and holidays, when many hotels offer discounts. If you have your heart set on a particular Denver hotel during the week, a reservation may mean the best room rate. Because many B&Bs have a limited number of rooms, it's not a bad idea to book ahead, particularly on weekends and during holiday seasons. Don't overlook the B&B reservation services if you're having trouble finding a place at the last minute. Of course, all prices listed are approximate and subject to change. If you book any accommodation using a credit card, ask the reservationist not to put the charge through until you actually show up. Unfortunately, credit card companies put a hold against your account for each reservation; that hold is often not lifted until a week or longer after you've checked out. This process can eat up your available credit. Tell the reservationist to simply keep your card number on file against the remote possibility that you won't show up; that way large holds won't mount up on your card. Incidentally, toll-free 800 numbers are a good way to save money. Since they seem to change frequently, don't despair if your call doesn't go through on the first try. Double-check by calling information at (800) 555-1212.

National and some state park camping sites are heavily booked. To avoid disappointment, check into your campground as early in the day as possible. Advance reservations are available at Yellowstone's Bridge Bay campground and Rocky Mountain National Park's Moraine Park and Glacier Basin campgrounds. They can be made for the summer season through Mistix, (800) 365-2267. In Colorado, you can also make state park reservations by calling Mistix at the same number. The Colorado Division of Parks and Outdoor Recreation at 1313 Sherman Street, Suite 618, Denver, CO 80203, is another good resource. Phone them at (303) 866-3437. For information on Wyoming state parks, phone (307) 777-7695. In Montana, state park information is available from (406) 444-2535; in Idaho, phone (208) 334-2154. Most campgrounds in this region open between early May and mid-June and shut down between early September and the end of October. Group reservations are available in many parks. Phone numbers and addresses are supplied in the appropriate lodging sections of this book. Many excellent national forest, county, and private campgrounds are also available in this popular region. Look for them whenever the national and state parks are at capacity.

Recommended Reading
For general background on this region, I recommend Francis Parkman's *The Oregon Trail* (New York: Penguin, 1982), *Stampede to Timberline* by Muriel Wolle (Denver: Sage, 1962), *The Strange Uncertain Years* by Amanda Mae Ellis (Hamden, Conn.: Shoestring Press, 1959), *Silver Dollar* by David Karsner (New York: Covici & Friede, 1932), and *Timber Line* by Gene Fowler (Sausalito: Comstock Editions, 1977). Gregory M. Franzwa's *The Oregon Trail Revisited* (St. Louis: Patrice Press, 1988) is an excellent mile-by-mile guide to this historic route and will enhance your visit to Wyoming. Another helpful general reference work is *Rocky Mountain States*, part of the *Smithsonian Guide to Historic America* (New York: Stewart Tabori & Chang, 1989).

The Colorado Guide* by Bruce Caughey and Dean Winstanley (Golden, Colo.: Fulcrum, 1989) is likely to be useful to you as you explore that state. For specific trail information, Lee Gregory's *Colorado Scenic Guides* (Boulder, Colo.: Johnson Publishing, 1983), covering the northern and southern regions, are both useful. The Historic Mining District Series, including concise guides to Durango and Silverton, the Georgetown-Silver Plume Historic District, as well as Central City and Black Hawk, are all recommended (Evergreen, Colo.: Cordillera Press, 1988). Charles S. Marsh's *People of the Shining Mountains* (Boulder, Colo.: Pruett, 1982) offers a first-rate history of the

Colorado Ute Indians, while Frank McNitt's *Richard Wetherill: Anasazi* (Albuquerque: University of New Mexico Press, 1966) tells the story of the discovery of the Mesa Verde cliff dwellings.

The Wyoming Recreation Commission's *Wyoming: Guide to Historic Sites* (Basin, Wyo.: Big Horn Book Company, 1976) is an essential traveling companion in that state. Every important landmark in the state is covered in detail, and the historic photographs are excellent. For background on the Teton region, try David J. Saylor's *Jackson Hole, Wyoming*, a comprehensive look at this mountain kingdom (Norman: University of Oklahoma Press, 1971). *Teton Trails* by Bryan Harry and *Short Hikes and Easy Walks in Grand Teton National Park* by Bill Hayden and Jerry Feilich are both useful, as is Tom Carter's *Day Hiking Yellowstone.* James Chisholm's *South Pass 1868: Journal of the Wyoming Gold Rush* (Lincoln: Bison Books, 1975) is a good account of the mining boom that created this famous city.

Carroll Van West's *A Traveler's Companion to Montana History* (Helena: Montana Historical Society Press, 1986) offers excellent background on this state's past and will enhance your visit. *Montana's Many-Splendored Glacierland* (Grand Forks: University of North Dakota Foundation, 1987) by Warren Hanna offers a comprehensive look at Glacier National Park.

Halka Chronic's *Pages of Stone*, vol. 1 (Seattle: The Mountaineers, 1988), is an excellent geologic guide to many of the highlights on your route including all the suggested national parks in the Rockies as well as Craters of the Moon, Dinosaur, and Fossil Butte national monuments. If you have an interest in bed and breakfasts, I recommend *The Complete Guide to Bed and Breakfasts, Inns and Guesthouses* (Berkeley, Cal.: Lanier Publications, 1993) by Pamela Lanier; it includes numerous suggestions across the Rockies as well as many B&B reservation services.

For current suggestions on restaurants, shows, and galleries, check the local publications such as the *Denver Post, Rocky Mountain News, Aspen Times,* or *Jackson Hole News.*

Landing the Big Ones

There's good fishing in the Rockies. Licenses are easily obtained at sporting goods stores, offices of outfitters, and state agencies. In Colorado, an annual fishing license is $35 for a nonresident, a 10-day license goes for $18, a 2-day license is $7, and a one-day license is $4. In Wyoming, a license for the season costs $35, while a 10-day nonresident license costs $20. In Montana, a nonresident license for the season is $37, while a 2-day license costs $10, plus $8 for each additional 2 days. Idaho fishing licenses cost nonresidents $36 for the season, $18 for 10 days, $11 for 3 days, and $6 for one day.

Tourist Boards

Colorado Tourism Board, 1625 Broadway, Suite 725, Denver, CO 80202; (303) 592-5510 or (800) 433-2656.

Wyoming Travel Commission, I-25 at College Drive, Cheyenne, WY 82002; (307) 777-7777 or (800) 225-5996.

Travel Montana, Department of Commerce, Helena MT 59620; (406) 444-2654 or (800) 541-1447.

Idaho Travel Council, Statehouse Mall, Boise, ID 83720; (208) 327-7444 or (800) 635-7820.

For a Safe Trip

A few simple precautions will help ensure your well-being on this trip. Millions of people visit here safely every year by following a few simple rules. Our itinerary encourages you to acclimate to the higher altitude by spending a day in Denver (5,200 feet) before heading up into the mountains. If you decide to begin your trip by flying directly to one of the high country resorts, take it easy for a day or two. Don't underestimate fast-changing weather conditions. Before heading out into wilderness areas, be sure to leave information on your route with a ranger station and be sure to carry necessary survival gear.

Researching this book, I saw some dramatic evidence of the ways freak winds can up-end RVs. You can avoid this problem by simply slowing down and using extra caution when driving over mountain passes. If you're uncertain how to protect yourself in this regard, check with any local police or highway patrol office. If you must drive at night, do so cautiously and watch for wild animals crossing the road. Children must remain under adult supervision at all times whenever you are near lakes and the fast-moving, often chilly streams that beautify this region. Why not equip your kids with whistles to help them signal you in the unlikely event you should become separated on the trail? Finally, don't succumb to the temptation to get close to the wildlife you'll see in the Rockies. Feeding these animals is unthinkable, and getting in close for a picture isn't wise. The deer, elk, moose, and buffalo, not to mention bear, can easily out-run you. Avoid the emergency room; keep your distance.

All the unpaved roads mentioned in this book are appropriate for cars and small RVs. If you are driving an oversized or wide vehicle or large RV, or towing anything, don't use any of these roads. Also, if you don't have experience with mountain driving, you may want to reconsider taking any dirt roads. In some cases, they lack guardrails and go along very steep dropoffs. If you have rented a vehicle, your insurance is invalid on dirt roads.

For current road condition information, call the numbers in these respective states as follows:

Colorado: (303) 639-1111; within two hours of Denver, (303) 639-1234

Montana: (800) 332-6171

Idaho: (208) 336-6600

Wyoming: (307) 635-9966

2 to 22 Days in the Rockies is a loop trip that focuses on the best of Colorado and Wyoming and includes a look at northeastern Utah. Additional extensions for travelers with more time lead to Montana and Idaho. Our suggested itineraries will help you set your priorities. But feel free to adapt our plan as you see fit.

For readers with less time who want to concentrate on a particular state or region, here are some ways to adapt the trip plan:

Colorado: Days 1-10 cover Denver, the Front Range, Central City, Georgetown, Aspen, Glenwood Springs, Lake City, Durango, Silverton, Mesa Verde, Dolores Canyon, and the Colorado National Monument. Days 20-22 cover Rocky Mountain National Park and Boulder. An itinerary extension at the end of this book includes Colorado Springs, Manitou Springs, Pikes Peak, Cripple Creek, Victor, Cañon City, and Royal Gorge.

Wyoming: Days 12-19 focus on the Grand Tetons, Yellowstone National Park, the Wind River Range, South Pass City, and the Medicine Bow National Forest.

Montana: Extension days include highlights such as Flathead Lake, the National Bison Range, Glacier National Park, the Blackfeet Indian Reservation, and the Lee Metcalf Wilderness.

Idaho: Extension days include the Sawtooth Wilderness, Sun Valley, and Craters of the Moon National Monument.

Utah: Day 11 covers the Utah side of Dinosaur National Monument and Flaming Gorge Reservoir.

If you don't have time to drive the entire itinerary, it's easy to connect by air to all major destinations in this region. Here are suggestions for short trips that will give you a good taste of the Rockies and where they can be found in this guide:

Denver: Days 1 and 22

Central City and Georgetown: Day 2

Rocky Mountain National Park: Days 20 and 21

Creede, Durango, Mesa Verde: Days 7-9

Dolores Canyon and Colorado National Monument: Day 10

Dinosaur National Monument: Day 11

Fort Bridger, Fossil Butte, Grand Tetons/Jackson Hole and Yellowstone National Park, Wyoming: Days 12-17

South Pass City: Day 18

Saratoga and Encampment, Wyoming: Day 19

Glacier National Park and other Montana highlights: Itinerary Extension

Sun Valley, Sawtooth National Recreation Area, and other Idaho highlights: Itinerary Extension

Colorado Springs region: Posttour Option

Oregon Trail: This book includes portions of the historic route being celebrated during its 150th anniversary year, 1993. See Days 12, 18, and 19.

22 Days in the Rockies

DAY 1   Arrive in Denver. Visit the Natural History Museum. Choose between Denver Art Museum, Museum of Western Art, or Black American West Museum. Lunch at 16th Street Mall. In the afternoon, visit the Colorado History Center and the Molly Brown House. Dinner and evening at Elitch Gardens Amusement Park or Larimer Square.

DAY 2   Head west to visit Buffalo Bill Cody's Grave and Memorial Museum. Continue on to the Central City/ Black Hawk historic district. See the Gilpin County Historical Museum, Carpenter Gothic Lace House, Teller House and Central City Opera House, and the Thomas Billings home. Optional Ride on Black Hawk and Central City Narrow Gauge Railroad. Take the Virginia Canyon

"Oh My God" Road south to Idaho Springs and head
west to Georgetown, where you'll spend the night.
Optional side trip to the top of Mount Evans.

DAY 3   After riding the Georgetown Loop railroad,
drive to the 10,000-foot-high mining capital of Leadville,
home of the famed Matchless Mine. Visit the historic
downtown, Healy House, and Tabor Opera House before
taking Independence Pass over the Continental Divide to
Aspen. After dinner, head over to the patio of the Jerome
Hotel for a drink.

DAY 4   Take a walking tour of Aspen, then hike Maroon
Lake Scenic Trail to Maroon Bells. Drive to Glenwood
Springs for a short rafting trip on the Colorado River, fol-
lowed by an evening dip in the giant Hot Springs Pool.
Overnight in Glenwood Springs.

DAY 5   Drive to Lake City via the old company towns of
Redstone and Marble, where stone was quarried for the
Lincoln Memorial. A cliff-hanging drive (don't worry, the
road is great) takes you along the Black Canyon of the
Gunnison before heading south to Lake City. Overnight
at a dude ranch or motel in Lake City.

DAY 6   In the morning, take a horseback or mountain
bike tour of the Lake City high country. Explore the
historic downtown and the pioneer museum and fish
local streams and rivers. This is the Colorado that dreams
are made of. Overnight in Lake City.

DAY 7   Drive south past the Rio Grande headwaters and
see the historic Creede mining district. Continue past
Pagosa Springs and Chimney Rock to one of the Rockies'
most picturesque communities, Durango. An optional
tour of Chimney Rock Archaeological Area can be
arranged with the Ute Indians. Enjoy the evening exploring historic Durango.

DAY 8   Nirvana for steam railroad enthusiasts: an all-day train ride on the Durango and Silverton Narrow Gauge Railroad. The trip recesses at midday in Silverton, where there's time to explore local museums and enjoy lunch. Or, if you prefer, take the Million Dollar Highway north to Silverton and Ouray, cut across to Telluride, and loop back to Durango.

DAY 9   The mecca of southwestern Colorado, Mesa Verde National Park is famous for its Anasazi cliff dwellings. This park is also distinguished by its hiking trails, museums, and panoramic vistas. Spend the night at Far View Lodge or a local campground. An optional extension takes you to another Ute Reservation archaeological zone, where you can visit little-known cliff dwellings with Indian guides.

DAY 10   Head north to the Anasazi Heritage Center in Dolores and then drive through an often overlooked red rock canyon to the Colorado National Monument. Overnight in Grand Junction.

DAY 11   Gone but not forgotten, the big guys are enshrined at today's focal point, the Utah side of Dinosaur National Park. Visit the dinosaur quarry, where you can see how the archaeological process works. Take the loop drive to visit the petroglyphs and historic ranches and hike along red sandstone cliffs and narrow gorges. Optional rafting trips on the Green and Yampa rivers run from half a day to five days. Spiral up the Uinta Mountains from Vernal and then drive down along Flaming Gorge Reservoir, one of the West's lesser-known scenic wonders. Spend the night in Green River, Wyoming.

DAY 12   Continue to historic Fort Bridger and Fossil Butte National Monument. After visiting Kemmerer, continue north across the Oregon Trail to the scenic Wind River Range and Jackson Hole, gateway to the Grand Tetons.

DAY 13 On your walking tour of Jackson, you'll visit Jackson Hole Museum, Teton County Historical Center, Wildlife of the American West Art Museum, and Town Square. After enjoying a picnic lunch at Jenny Lake, you'll hike to String and Leigh lakes. Then you'll continue on to Colter Bay Indian Arts Museum, one of the region's finest Native American collections, before returning to town to enjoy the town shootout, a rodeo, music festival, or play.

DAY 14 Today you'll take a float trip down the Snake River, enjoy panoramic views of the Tetons, and spot some of the park's famous wildlife. In the afternoon you'll take a ferry across Jenny Lake to Hidden Falls and continue up to Inspiration Point for a panoramic view of the Jackson Hole region.

DAY 15 A two-hour drive north takes you to one of America's most important geologic treasures, Yellowstone National Park. After orienting yourself at the visitor center, step out for a look at Old Faithful, the geyser that seems to be slowly losing its steam, and then wander through the thermal wonders of Upper and Lower Geyser Basins. Explore the Dantelike world of boiling caldrons, mud pots and steam vents, dodging the hot showers that come without warning; then, for dinner, visit one of the national park system's best-loved hostelries, Old Faithful Inn.

DAY 16 Your day begins with a visit to the 1988 Fire Exhibition and continues on to Lake Yellowstone Hotel. From here it's an easy hike along the Yellowstone Lake shore for views of waterfowl and mammals. Then visit the museum at Fishing Bridge and drive north to see Mud Volcano, Black Dragon's Caldron, Artist Point, and Inspiration Point. Your day is completed with one of the Rockies' grandest adventures, a pleasant hike down into the colorful Grand Canyon of the Yellowstone.

DAY 17   Continue north to see Yellowstone's photogenic Tower Fall. From here you'll head west to see a sight that has been dazzling visitors to this park for more than a century: the limestone terraces of Mammoth Hot Springs. Also included is a visit to the Norris Geyser Basin. Finish the day by driving through the burn mosaic left by the 1988 fire and getting a chance to photograph elk, moose, deer, and buffalo at a distance.

Optional Extension: Montana/Idaho   This 10-day side trip shows you some of the highlights of these states in a convenient loop that begins at Yellowstone National Park and rejoins the main itinerary on Day 18. Drive through southwestern Montana to the old mining towns of Virginia City and Nevada City, then continue to Butte's historic district. After a stop in the copper capital of Anaconda, you'll see the Grant-Kohrs Ranch National Historic Site and the famous ghost town of Garnet, as well as Missoula. Other Montana highlights include the U.S. Smoke Jumpers Center, National Bison Range, Glacier National Park, Bob Scriver Gallery/Museum in Browning, Kalispell/Whitefish, Flathead Lake, Lee Metcalf Wildlife Preserve, and the palatial Daly Mansion in the Bitterroot Mountains. Cross over into Idaho and drive along the Salmon River to see the handsome ghost towns of Sunbeam and Bonanza. After a visit to one of the prettiest mountain regions in the United States, the Sawtooth National Recreation Area, drive on into Sun Valley and the Ketchum resort area, where you can see Hemingway's grave. Visit the weird volcanic landscape of Craters of the Moon National Monument and then return to Wyoming and the main itinerary.

DAY 18   Drive southeast along the Wind River Range to the Wind River Indian Reservation at Fort Washakie. Continue on to South Pass City, the famous mining town that was also an Oregon Trail crossroads. You'll have a chance to explore museums, period homes, and monuments to the great western migration. Spend the night in this meticulously restored Wyoming town or at nearby Atlantic City, where you can enjoy dinner at a charming restaurant most western visitors miss.

DAY 19   Drive south to the Oregon Trail landmark of Split Rock and then continue to Medicine Bow National Forest. You'll visit the restored copper mining town of Grand Encampment and enjoy a dip in Saratoga Hot Springs. Fishermen will enjoy trying their skills on the North Platte.

DAY 20   Drive to Rocky Mountain National Park. After exploring the venerable Kauffman House, take a hike on the Colorado River Trail or go for a boat ride on aptly named Grand Lake. In the evening, enjoy a ranger talk or go stargazing.

DAY 21   Cross the Continental Divide via Trail Ridge Road, the ultimate transalpine drive. En route, stop at Never Summer Ranch and the Alpine Visitors Center. Then hike to Mills Lake and Jewel Lake before checking into a lodge or campground on the east side of the park. In the evening, take in a play at the Stanley Hotel Theater.

DAY 22   Drive back to Denver via the Peak to Peak Highway and the college town of Boulder. Enjoy lunch and street performers on the Pearl Street Mall. See Fiske Planetarium, and, if time permits, take a walking tour of Mapleton Hill. Then return to Denver, where you may have time to pick up any of the options you missed on Day 1. Check into your hotel and begin your homeward journey the following day.

Posttour Option: Colorado Springs Area   This three-day trip begins with a visit to the Broadmoor, Cheyenne Mountain Zoo, and the Pikes Peak Cog Railway. On the second day, you'll drive through the old resort community of Manitou Springs to the Garden of the Gods Park and then visit the Cripple Creek and Victor mining district. Mine tours, a historic railway ride, and museums bring the story of this great boomtown back to life. Then return to Colorado Springs via Phantom Canyon and Cañon City. On your last day, you can visit the Air Force Academy, Pro Rodeo Hall of Fame, the historic McAllister House, and our North American Air Defense Command base.

DAY 1
DENVER

They're still minting money in Denver, your gateway to the Rockies. Before heading up into the Front Range, you'll have a chance to learn something about this town built on the spoils of the old mining empires that colonized this region.

You'll also learn about the area's natural, political, and artistic heritage. A visit to one of America's finest natural history museums is followed by a stop at the estimable Colorado History Museum and lunch on the outside patio of the Denver Art Museum. In the afternoon you'll be able to visit the Denver Mint, the Museum of Western Art, or the Black American West Museum. In the evening see one of America's finest pre-Disney amusement parks.

Suggested Schedule

9:00 a.m.	Denver Natural History Museum.
11:30 a.m.	Colorado History Museum.
1:00 p.m.	Lunch at Denver Art Museum.
2:00 p.m.	Choose between Denver Mint and State Capitol.
3:30 p.m.	Choose between Museum of Western Art and Black American West Museum.
5:30 p.m.	Evening at Elitch Gardens Amusement Park.

Denver

Many words leap to mind when you alight in Denver, but the one that seems to sum up this metropolitan area of 1.8 million is "inexhaustible." From trendy Larimer Square downtown (a standing joke here is the plan to open a mortuary called "Death and Things") to the summer magic of Elitch Gardens, an old-time amusement park, the city is a year-round magnet for knowledgeable travelers. Less than two hours from some of the nation's premier mountain resorts, the city is also a popular gateway for dude ranch trips, rafting, hiking, climbing, steam

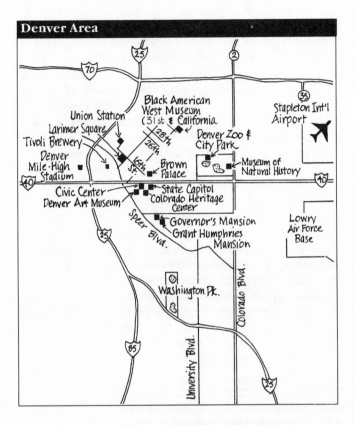

Denver Area

rail adventures, four-wheel high country drives, and
ghost town visits. In an hour you can reach Georgetown
or the famed Gold Rush boomtown of Central City—
both on the Day 2 itinerary. And to the south are the Air
Force Academy, Colorado Springs, Pikes Peak, and the
Cripple Creek/Victor mining district (see Posttour
Option, pp. 175-182). As the region's central air hub, the
city offers direct connections to all of the intermountain
West's principal resort destinations.

Denver was created in the 1859 "Pikes Peak or Bust"
gold rush at the confluence of the South Platte River and
Cherry Creek. The original frontier town was tamed by
the new mining barons who came down from the gold

and silver camps to build broad boulevards and line them with ostentatious mansions. Located on a mile-high plateau, 12 miles east of the Front Range of the Rockies, this city offers pleasant bikeways, verdant parks, and museums. This state capital became the hub of the emerging Rocky Mountain region and its oil and gas industry. The collapse of the oil shale business and a decline in the energy industry have hurt the city's business community. But Denver remains a thriving tourist destination thanks to its proximity to the dry powder of the Rocky Mountain resorts. A dry climate that makes the community a near desert (rainfall here is about 15 inches a year, the same as Los Angeles) makes Denver and the surrounding region a popular retreat during the warm weather months.

Denver is a natural jump-off point for a three-week tour of the Rockies, and its museums offer a good overview of the region you're about to explore. This is also an excellent city for families, thanks to its grand roller coasters, children's museums, sports centers, and, of course, the Denver Mint. Enjoy your visit and prepare yourself for the cliff-hanging landscape that begins tomorrow morning.

Arrival

Stapleton Airport, 7 miles east of downtown, and the Amtrak Station in the heart of Denver are both convenient gateways to the Mile High City. In addition to the major car rental firms, I've had good luck with Enterprise (800-325-8007) and Payless (800-231-5537). When shopping around for a car before leaving home, be sure to look for an unlimited mileage deal, or you may get hit with a hefty surcharge for your trip. Remember that if you are abbreviating this itinerary, taking a one-way trip and dropping your car at a city other than Denver, you'll want to compare prices carefully. The size of the drop charge may be the most important factor in your rental decision. Don't hesitate to ask for a free upgrade on your vehicle size when you sign your contract. Depending on availability, counter agents may be happy to oblige you. I recommend taking the collision damage waiver if you don't have full coverage through another source. If you're planning to rent an RV for your trip, it still makes sense to rent a car for your first day and rent the RV on Day 2. That way you'll enjoy the convenience of a more maneuverable vehicle on the first day in Denver. From the airport, the easiest way to reach the downtown area is to take Martin Luther King Boulevard (East 32nd) to Colorado Boulevard and turn left. Turn right on Colfax and head west into the heart of the city. You may find it more convenient to take a $10 taxi ride to your hotel, the Airporter bus, a shared limo, or the city bus that departs near door 5 on the airport terminal's lower level. Incidentally, there is also a visitor information center at Stapleton Airport located between the C and D concourses.

If you're arriving by car from the east or west via I-70, exit on I-25 southbound and take the Colfax Avenue (Highway 40/287) exit into downtown. Travelers coming from the north or south will enter Denver on I-25 and take the same downtown exit on Colfax. A good initial destination is the Denver Metro Convention and Visitors Bureau at 225 West Colfax Avenue, Denver, CO 80202, (303) 892-1112.

Bus and Taxi: The Regional Transportation District offers public transit for the Denver/Boulder region. Call 299-6000 for schedule information. Free shuttle buses leaving from both ends of the 16th Street Mall downtown are a convenient way to explore the central city. For taxi service, call Yellow Cab at 777-7777.

Lodging

Although a downtown location is most convenient for your Day 1 travel plan, I've also suggested a number of other possibilities in other parts of town. When booking, keep in mind that many establishments offer substantial discounts on weekends. Even top hotels offer rooms in the $60 range on Friday and Saturday nights. Downtown, the venerable **Brown Palace Hotel** at 321 17th Street has fine rooms and a central location. Rates range from $149 to $225. (303) 297-3111. In the same price range is the smaller all-suite **Burnsley Hotel** at 1000 Grant. (303)

830-1000. Another expensive downtown hotel with comfortable suites is the **Cambridge Hotel** at 1560 Sherman Street. (303) 831-1252. Close to Denver's Union Station at 1600 17th Street is the **Oxford Alexis Hotel**. Listed on the National Register of Historic Places, this restored landmark is popular with guests taking the ski train to Winter Park. Rooms run $60 to $140. (303) 628-5400. South of downtown near the Cherry Creek Shopping Center is **Loews Giorgio Hotel** at 4150 E. Mississippi. Rooms run $125 to $145. (303) 782-9300 or (800) 223-0888. The **Scanticon Denver Hotel** at 200 Inverness Drive West in Englewood about 20 minutes south of downtown is the only hotel in Denver with a golf course and tennis courts attached. Rates are $69 to $119. (303) 799-5800 or (800) 346-4891. In the $50 to $65 range is the **Comfort Inn** at 401 17th Street. (303) 296-0400. The **Best Western Landmark Inn** at 455 South Colorado Boulevard at Cherry Creek Shopping Center south of downtown charges $59 to $185. (303) 388-5561. Rooms at the **Cherry Creek Inn**, 600 South Colorado Boulevard, run $55 to $78. (303) 757-3341.

B&Bs: The **Queen Anne Inn**, a bed and breakfast at 2147 Tremont Place downtown, runs $59 to $125. (303) 296-6666. Also downtown in the same price range is the **Victoria Oaks Inn** at 1575 Race Street. (303) 355-1818. **Seventh Avenue Manor** at 722 East 7th Avenue offers rooms for $55 to $150. (303) 832-0039. For B&B reservations in Denver and the rest of the region, call B&B Rocky Mountains at (800) 825-0225, or write to P.O. Box 804, Colorado Springs, CO 80901, for a free brochure. Or call Bed and Breakfast Colorado Ltd., (303) 494-4994, for information on many other Colorado B&Bs. For a list of historic hotels, call the Association of Historic Hotels of the Rocky Mountain West, (800) 626-4886.

Budget: Denver International Youth Hostel at 630 E. 16th Avenue offers dorm beds for $6. Bring your own sleeping bag. (303) 832-9996. Incidentally, the American Youth Hostels Rocky Mountain Council at P.O. Box 2370, Boulder, CO 80306, can refer you to hostels in a dozen other Colorado cities. Phone (303) 442-1166.

Food
Downtown: For expensive continental dining downtown, try **Cliff Young's** at 700 E. 17th Avenue, (303) 831-8900. A good choice for northern Italian is **Al Fresco** at 1523 Market Street, (303) 534-0404. The **Margarita Bay Club**, 1301 South Pearl Street, (303) 871-0603, offers fine Mexican food at moderate prices. The back patio is a good place to dine in warm weather. The historic **Buckhorn Exchange** at 1000 Osage is the place to dine on buffalo and steaks as stuffed animals look over your shoulder. (303) 534-9505. **Le Central, the Affordable French Restaurant** on 8th Avenue at Lincoln, lives up to its name with good inexpensive continental fare. (303) 863-8094. For upscale Chinese, try **Imperial Chinese** at 1 Broadway, (303) 698-2800.

Elsewhere in Denver: White Fence Farm, about 20 minutes southeast of downtown at 6263 Jewell Avenue, serves moderately priced chicken dinners family style. A small farm and antique shop make this one especially popular with children. To avoid a wait, arrive early. (303) 935-5945. For a superior steak, try **Aurora Summit**, 2700 South Havana on the southeast side of town. (303) 751-2112. Good Mexican food is available at **El Noa Noa**, 722 Santa Fe Drive. (303) 623-9968. Between Cherry Creek and Denver University, the **Bonnie Brae Tavern** at 740 S. University is a popular pizza spot. (303) 777-2262. On the north side, **Brittney Hill** at 9350 Grant off I-25 in Thornton offers a great view of the Rockies and good prime rib in an elegant setting. (303) 451-5151.

Sightseeing Highlights
▲▲▲**Denver Natural History Museum**—Drive east from downtown on Colfax and turn left on Colorado Boulevard to City Park. One of the finest museums of its kind in the country, this collection just ten minutes from downtown is a perfect introduction to the natural world you are about to see. A recent $20 million renovation has added several new exhibits, including three towering dinosaurs. Among them is a *Tyrannosaurus rex* that

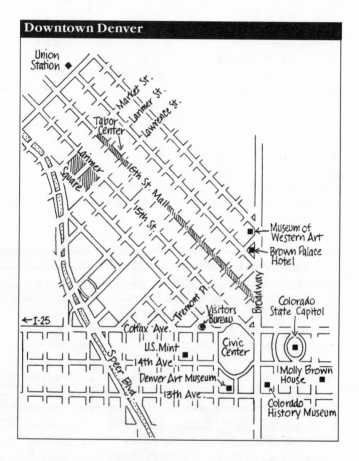

Downtown Denver

receives visitors at the front door. The vast Indian collection here extends from the Alaskan Eskimos to Florida's Seminoles. At the Coors Mineral Hall you'll see a fine display of Colorado gold and gemstones. Included is a subterranean cavern with rocks illuminated by fluorescent lighting. In addition, there are nearly 90 dioramas featuring plants, birds, butterflies, and animals from around the world, a Hall of Life health education center, a planetarium (featuring laser and rock shows), and an IMAX theater with a giant six-story screen. Permanent collections cover the flora and fauna, geology, and wildlife of the Rockies. Be sure not to miss the museum's most unique

exhibit, the blue whale skeleton. The museum is open
daily 9:00 a.m. to 9:00 p.m. (303) 322-7009. Admission is
$4 for adults; $2 for seniors and children ages 4 to 12. For
IMAX and planetarium/laser show times and prices, call
(303) 370-6300.

▲▲**Colorado History Museum**—Turn right on
Colorado Boulevard, right on Colfax to Broadway, and
left to 13th Avenue. Although the collection focuses on
Colorado, you'll also learn a good deal about the history
of the entire Rocky Mountain region. A time line guides
you from early days of the cliff-dwelling Anasazi Indians,
through pioneer settlements, the gold rush era, and the
legendary scandals of Horace and Baby Doe Tabor (more
on this nineteenth-century soap opera on Day 3; be sure
not to miss Baby Doe's $7,000 wedding dress on display
here at the History Center). Special exhibits include mining tools, equipment, and machinery, an authentic sod
house, a gold rush-era log cabin, and Indian artifacts. The
museum is open Monday through Saturday 10:00 a.m. to
4:30 p.m. and on Sunday 12:00 noon to 4:30 p.m. Admission is $3 for adults and $1.50 for seniors and children
ages 5 to 15. (303) 866-3682.

▲**Denver Art Museum**—Walk west on 14th Avenue
one block to the Denver Art Museum. This 28-sided
building, located at 100 W. 14th Avenue Parkway, resem-
bles a medieval fortress. Home of one of the West's most
important art collections, this museum is best known for
its recently renovated American Indian Hall. The 20,000-
piece collection, valued at more than $25 million,
spans more than 2,000 years. Artworks from more than
150 U.S. and Canadian tribes are represented, and the collection is particularly strong on Northwest Indian pieces.
Among the highlights is the one-of-a-kind Shakes Screen,
a large carved and painted panel depicting the family
crest of the Shake family of Wrangell, Alaska. Also here is
the Wiyot tribe basketry of Elizabeth Hickox and a water
jar by one of the world's best-known potters, Maria Marti-
nez of San Ildefonso Pueblo, New Mexico. In addition to
this collection of Indian pottery, headdresses, and
basketry, a two-story atrium exhibits totem poles. Also

found here are Asian and Spanish-American works as well as paintings by Picasso and Monet. Thomas Cole's *Dream of Arcadia* is one of the collection's American classics. The patio is a great spot for lunch on a sunny day. A good time to visit is Wednesday evening, when you can enjoy the exhibits and live music. Hours are Tuesday through Saturday 10:00 a.m. to 5:00 p.m. and Sunday 12:00 noon to 5:00 p.m. Closed Mondays and holidays. (303) 575-2793. Admission is $3 for adults, $1.50 for seniors and students.

▲ **United States Mint**—Walk west on 14th Avenue to Cherokee Street. If there are children in your party, they'll definitely want to tour the United States Mint, an Italian Renaissance building holding America's second-largest gold bullion supply. On your 20-minute tour, you'll gaze down from elevated walkways to see how spare change is created at this facility, which stamps out $5 billion worth of coins annually. The gift shop at the end of the tour is an ideal place to pick up souvenirs of your visit. Tours are conducted weekdays 8:00 a.m. to 3:00 p.m., except Wednesday when tours begin at 9:00 a.m. Naturally, there's no admission charge. (303) 844-3582.

▲ **State Capitol**—Walk east on Colfax to 1475 Sherman Street. With its beautiful gold dome, vaulted ceilings, and stained glass, this building is downtown's architectural centerpiece. From the top story you'll get a good view of the Front Range. Free tours that begin at the west entrance are offered weekdays from 9:00 a.m. to 3:00 p.m.

▲ **Black American West Museum**—Take Lincoln north to Stout Street and turn right to 31st Street. Then turn left to California. The museum is located on the corner at 3091 California Street. It is one of Denver's authentic treasures, a fascinating collection on the largely over-looked story of the black American cowboy. You'll learn that at least 25 percent of the cowboys who helped tame the West were nonwhite. Most of the black cowboys were part of the western mainstream, working cattle, tending horses, and creating their own ranches. Historian Paul Stewart has also documented two communities settled by

Metropolitan Denver

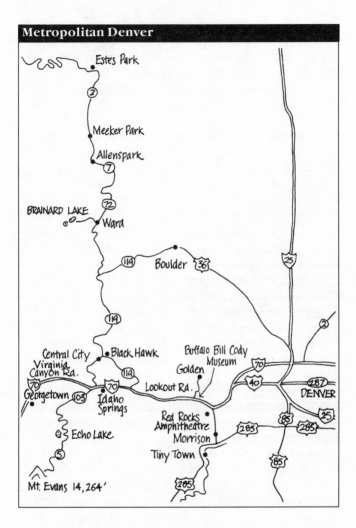

blacks: Nicodemus, Kansas, and Deerfield, Colorado. Many of the black pioneers who helped settle the West were emancipated slaves who broke into the cattle business with considerable experience from the plantations and ranches. Since the Civil War had decimated the economy of the southern states, free black men were ideal recruits for the often dangerous business of herding cattle on long drives.

In addition to the story of cowboys like rodeo star Bill Pickett, who was famous for leaping out of his saddle and gripping a steer by sinking his teeth into the animal's lips, the museum has memorialized cowgirls. Among them is Mary Fields, a slave who escaped the plantation in 1832 and tried to break into the restaurant business. Her tendency to overextend credit and then punch out deadbeats helped put her dining establishment under. She did better riding shotgun on a stagecoach and eventually became the second woman in American history to deliver the U.S. mail. Stewart's museum and the book *Black Cowboys*, which he wrote with Wallace Yvonne Ponce (Broomfield, Colo.: Phillips Publishing, 1986), also look at the careers of black outlaws like Ned Huddleston, better known as Isom Dart. Drifting in and out of horse rustling, he made several unsuccessful attempts to go straight. After being arrested in Brown's Hole, Wyoming, the suspect and a deputy sheriff had a stage accident. Thanks to nursing skills learned as a slave in Arkansas, the unhurt Dart revived the unconscious deputy and then rushed the lawman to a hospital. The jury was so impressed by Dart's selflessness that he was acquitted. The museum is open Wednesday through Friday 10:00 a.m. to 2:00 p.m., Saturday 10:00 a.m. to 5:00 p.m., and Sunday 2:00 p.m. to 5:00 p.m. (303) 292-2566. After leaving this museum, drive back on California to Broadway to 1727 Tremont Place.

▲**Museum of Western Art**—You don't have to live out West or be a student of western art to appreciate the significance of the works of painters and sculptors like Henry Farney, Charles Russell, Albert Bierstadt, Frederic Remington, and Georgia O'Keeffe. By stepping into this former Denver bordello, you can share the vision of many of the great names in western art. This collection across the way from the Brown Palace Hotel is a Who's Who of western art. Paintings include Remington's *Downing the Nigh Leader*, Maynard Dixon's *Spring Plowing*, and Thomas Hart Benton's *After Many Springs*. Located in the old Navarre Hotel, the museum exhibits these classics in a series of galleries built around a central atrium. Clearly the collection is dedicated to the cowboy, the mythic American hero Russell characterized as "the man who could tell you what a cow said to her calf. The floor of his home was the prairie, the sky his roof which often leaked. His gift of God was his health and he generally cashed in with his boots on. He was only part human but always liked animals." The museum is open Tuesday through Saturday 10:00 a.m. to 4:30 p.m. (303) 296-1880. Admission is $3 for adults, $1.50 for seniors and youths ages 6 to 15. After leaving the museum, take Colfax west to I-25 north. Exit at 38th Avenue and drive west to Tennyson Street.

▲▲ **Elitch Gardens**— B.D. (Before Disney) amusement parks were family-style places known for their rides, theaters, and picnic grounds. This century-old Denver tradition is a great way to wind up your first day in the Rockies. Thrill rides include a historic wooden roller coaster, the Twister, and the smaller Wild Cat. You can enjoy the flume ride, roll about in the Round Up, enjoy the turn-of-the-century carousel, and get a good view of the Front Range from the Sky Ride. Musical revues, jugglers, and magicians keep the crowd entertained at this beautifully landscaped park. Ornamented with colorful flower beds, Elitch's should be designated a national historic landmark. The park, located at 4620 W. 38th Avenue, is open May though Labor Day. (303) 455-4771. From mid-June to late August, it's open Sunday through Thursday 10:00 a.m. to 9:00 p.m., Friday and Saturday 10:00 a.m. to 10:00 p.m. From late May to mid-June, the park is open Friday from 5:00 p.m. to 11:00 p.m., Saturday from 10:00 a.m. to 11:00 p.m., and Sunday from 10:00 a.m. to 10:00 p.m. During the last week of August, hours are Monday through Friday 5:00 p.m. to 10:00 p.m. Labor Day weekend, the park is open 10:00 a.m. to 11:00 p.m. Unlimited ride tickets are $10.50 for adults and $7.95 to $8.50 for children.

Other Sights
Here are some other excellent possibilities for visitors who have extra time in Denver.

▲ **Larimer Square**—Adaptive reuse, a fancy way of describing the conversion of old neighborhoods into night spots, shopping malls, and restaurants, is much in evidence in downtown. You can find it at the Tivoli Denver (9th and Larimer streets), the 16th Street Mall, Tabor Center, and here in the Denver development that helped launch the downtown revival. This is a pleasant spot to dine, go to the theater, window shop, and perhaps buy. If you're not going to Elitch's tonight, by all means consider strolling through this downtown district located in the 1400 block of Larimer Street.

▲ **Children's Museum**—This is a good bet for families. The museum is filled with handsome exhibits, play areas, art classes, scientific displays, a jungle display, music and puppet shows, and a room where kids can swim amidst 80,000 plastic balls. To reach this museum, take Exit 211 off I-25. The address is 2121 Crescent Drive. The museum is open daily 10:00 a.m. to 5:00 p.m. June through August. During the balance of the year, hours are 10:00 a.m. to 5:00 p.m. Tuesday through Sunday. Admission is $3 on weekdays and $2.50 on weekends in the summer. The rest of the year, admission is $2.50 on weekdays and $3 on weekends. (303) 433-7444.

▲ **Washington Park**—This is a great place to take the kids. There are duck ponds, paddleboats, indoor swimming pools, bicycle trails, and beautiful gardens, a great place to unwind for all members of the family. Bring a picnic lunch. The park is just fifteen minutes from downtown, on the south side of the city on Downing Street near East Alameda Avenue. Take the Alameda Avenue exit east off I-25 and then turn right on Downing Street to the park.

▲ **Celebrity Sports Center**—Hey kids! Thanks for reading along with your parents and patiently touring with them. Now it's your turn to enjoy one of Denver's great treasures. If you're looking for a water slide park that also has an Olympic-size swimming pool, 80 bowling lanes, skee ball, and over 300 video games, I have just the place. It's located at 888 South Colorado Boulevard. You'll be able to entertain yourself here for hours while the grownups go their own separate way. Just be sure to bring quarters. Lots of them. (303) 757-3321.

▲**Molly Brown House**—Located downtown at 1340 Pennsylvania, this Victorian monument commemorates the unsinkable wife of mining baron J. J. Brown. Molly, who emerged as a hero during the *Titanic* tragedy, was portrayed by Debbie Reynolds in the silver screen story of her life. Docents in period costumes offer guided tours 10:00 a.m. to 4:00 p.m. Tuesday through Saturday and noon to 4:00 p.m. on Sunday from May to September. The rest of the year hours are 10:00 a.m. to 3:00 p.m. Tuesday through Saturday and 12:00 to 3:00 p.m. on Sunday. Admission is $3 for adults and $1.50 for seniors and youths ages 6 to 18. (303) 832-4092.

▲**Grant Humphreys Mansion**—Located at 770 Pennsylvania Street, just a few blocks from the Molly Brown House, this eclectic 42-room home was built in 1902 for former governor James Grant. On your tour you'll see the bowling alley, billiard room, and a remarkable 10-car garage. Hours are Tuesday through Friday 10:00 a.m. to 2:00 p.m. Admission is $2 for adults and $1 for seniors and youths ages 6 to 16. (303) 894-2505.

DENVER TO CENTRAL CITY AND GEORGETOWN

Yesterday they formed the scenic backdrop to your Denver visit. Today you ascend the Front Range for your first look at North America's premier mountain range. Compared favorably with peaks throughout the world, the Rockies are a magical place at any time of year. Driving through steep-walled river canyons, looking at dinosaur footprints in red rock sandstone fossil beds, and ascending to the top of a 14,000-foot peak are just a few of the fringe benefits of this, your first day in the mountains.

Suggested Schedule

9:00 a.m.	Leave Denver.
10:00 a.m.	Visit Tiny Town.
11:30 a.m.	Visit Buffalo Bill Cody Museum and Grave.
1:00 p.m.	See Black Hawk's Lace House and then drive to Central City.
4:00 p.m.	"Oh My God" Road through Virginia Canyon.
5:30 p.m.	Arrive Georgetown.
Evening	At leisure.

Travel Route: Denver to Georgetown via Central City (135 miles)

Take I-25 south to US 85 south (Santa Fe Drive). Continue to US 285 west toward the mountains. About 5 miles past the Morrison exit, you'll pass mile marker 246 and see the Tiny Town exit sign that leads up Turkey Creek Road. Return to Morrison via Colorado 8 north and then pick up Hogback Road north to Interstate 70 westbound. Take exit 256 and follow Lookout Mountain Road to the cutoff for the Cody Grave and Museum. Return to Interstate 70, continue westbound to exit 244, and pick up Colorado 119 to Black Hawk. Continue on Colorado 279 to Central City. Return to Idaho Springs by the rugged Virginia Canyon ("Oh My God" Road) route that begins by taking Spring Street south from Central City. If you prefer a less serpentine route, are driving an oversize vehicle, or are uncomfortable on a cliff-hanging mountain road, double back east on Colorado 279 and Colorado 119 south to Interstate 70 westbound to Georgetown, exit 228. With the exception of the Virginia Canyon route, these are all good mountain roads. The steep grade up I-70 from Hog-back Road gives you a chance to check out your horse-power in the high country.

The Rockies
Under construction for the past 1,750 million years, the Rockies have been beautifully sculpted by earthquake faults and glaciation. Every year this mountain wilderness delights millions of visitors who come to explore its alpine forests, river canyons, rugged passes, lakes, and tundra above the timberline. In her book on this region, *Pages of Stone* (Seattle: The Mountaineers, 1988), Halka Chronic calls geology "history, or prehistory, a course without lectures, with the Earth for its textbook." As you travel the Rockies, you'll learn about the three classes of rocks: sedimentary, deposited on ancient sea floors; igneous, created by hot magma that erupted from volcanoes; and metamorphic, created by heat and pressure within the earth itself. You'll see the fossils that tell the story of prehistoric species as well as primitive pictographs written on tablets of stone. Nearly every day you'll have a chance to take another geology lesson at the hands of rangers, guides, museum docents, or other experts. While you'll certainly want to play, relax, swim, sun yourself, and explore the handiwork of some of the region's earliest settlers, it is the Rockies themselves that remain at the heart of your journey. Beginning today we'll try to help by pointing out some of the memorable landmarks that all too many visitors to this region pass at 70 mph.

Sightseeing Highlights
▲▲ **Tiny Town**—Once second only to Pikes Peak as a Colorado tourist destination, Tiny Town, a mini city on

the edge of the Front Range, was founded in 1915 by moving company owner George Turner. Originally just a playhouse built for his daughter, the town soon grew into a 125-building village complete with its own miniature railroad. A series of disasters including floods and a fire turned this little community into the West's first mini ghost town. Thanks to the volunteer efforts of the people of nearby Morrison, the town has been restored and re-opened. If you have children in your group, don't even think about skipping this fun spot. They will love explor-ing this little village that includes a replica of an old Den-ver fire station, a hotel, a church, a poolroom, and min-ing buildings. Just 18 miles from Denver, Tiny Town is located at 6249 S. Turkey Creek Road. It's open daily June through September from 10:00 a.m. to 7:00 p.m. and weekends in May and October from 10:00 a.m. to 5:00 p.m. (303) 790-9393. Admission is $2 for adults and $1 for seniors and children ages 5 to 12. The train ride is $1. For more information on Tiny Town, be sure to read Carla Black's article in the August 1989 issue of *Ameri-cana* magazine.

Return to Morrison via US 285 and Colorado 8, where you can enjoy dinner at the Fort, 19192 Highway 8. (303) 697-4771. This town is a pleasant place to shop for antiques, and you can also dine here at the Morrison Inn, 301 Highway 74. (303) 697-6650. As you drive north on Hogback Road you'll come to Red Rocks Park, a popular local concert venue. Acoustics in this natural amphithe-ater are so perfect that someone sitting at the top of the bleachers can hear a coin or Ping-Pong ball dropped on the stage. This will be your first look at the red sandstone that adds so much beauty to the Rockies. Just half a mile east of Red Rocks is the Hogback, an impressive forma-tion where archaeologists found the state's biggest dino-saur skeleton. Take a close look at the rock and you'll spot dinosaur footprints.

▲▲**Buffalo Bill's Grave and Museum**—Queen City of the Plains, home of Coors beer, and the community that made plutonium triggers for nuclear weapons, Denver has many claims to fame. Among them is the city's stature as the final resting place of the Wild West's greatest show-man, Buffalo Bill Cody. The gravesite and Buffalo Bill Memorial Museum are reached by taking exit 256 off I-70 and ascending to the top of 7,500-foot-high Lookout Mountain. Like the road to the summit of Mont St. Michel, this is one of those pilgrimages that you'll remember for years to come. Not far from the city's resident buffalo herd at Genesee Park, this memorial tells the story of the last of the great American scouts, a man who lived in a tent for 60 years as he rode the West and then memorialized it in his legendary road show. "No one can deny that Cody excelled as a guide, sharpshooter, horse-man, endurance rider, hunter, stagecoach driver, and army scout," says Stan Zamonski, author of *Buffalo Bill, the Man and the Museum* (Frederick, Colo.: Renaissance House, 1986). "Perhaps the greatest showman of his era, he likely could have been elected president." This museum offers a look at the story of Cody's career as a Pony Express rider, army scout, buffalo hunter, and showman. Exhibits feature memorabilia from his shows and period artwork.

Born in Iowa in 1847, Cody went to work as a wagon train messenger at 11, and two years later joined the Colorado gold rush. After failing in the mining business, he became a wagon master and, at the age of 14, America's youngest Pony Express rider. When one of his fellowmen was shot down by an Indian, Cody rode 21 horses for 322 miles on a grueling 24-hour ride. He went on to serve as an army scout and then became a legend-ary Kansas Pacific Railroad buffalo hunter, helping to feed work crews by single-handedly reducing the buffalo population by 4,289. In the museum you'll see exhibits on Cody's Indian battles, his heroic rescues of snow-bound troops, and his efforts to defend settlers, which made him an American folk hero.

It was Cody who rode 190 miles in 58 hours as a vital messenger in the 1868 war against the Kiowa and Comanche. It was Cody who guided the Fifth Cavalry into position for their victory over the Cheyenne in July 1869. And after the debacle at Little Big Horn, it was

Cody who scalped the legendary warrior Yellow Hand, crying in victory, "First scalp for Custer."

Buffalo Bill became a national hero who spent his summers working for the army and winters acting out his famed battles for packed houses. Visiting this collection, you'll learn about the show that gradually became a Wild West extravaganza with a cast of 640, including a number of the Indians who fought him on the battlefield.

As Cody's entourage grew, he began traveling abroad with his performers, 180 horses, elk, deer, buffalo, and Texas longhorn steers. Buffalo Bill's Wild West and Congress of Rough Riders was a big hit with Queen Victoria, Pope Leo XIII, and Kaiser Wilhelm, who had a cigarette shot from his lips by Annie Oakley. The show continued to grow and added more acts as Cody became the first circus operator to give women the same billing and pay received by men. While this enterprise earned as much as $1 million a year, the crack shot was a naive businessman, constantly being bilked by unscrupulous entrepreneurs. After 30 years, the show was ultimately liquidated at a sheriff's sale, with cowboys and Indians alike forced to sell their costumes and weapons to finance trips back home. Even Cody's favorite horse, Isham, was auctioned off, although the buyer turned out to be a friend who returned the mount in a gesture of respect.

Buffalo Bill died in 1917. But even after his burial, the scout remained a controversial figure. Zamonski writes that citizens of Cody, Wyoming, were determined to transfer his remains to their city. In 1948 the Cody American Legion Post offered a $10,000 cash reward "for the return of Buffalo Bill's body from Colorado to Cody." Denver citizens promptly responded by dispatching matching tanks up Lookout Mountain. With armed guards standing watch, Denver officials exhumed the body and replaced the coffin with a 3-inch-thick casing. Cody was laid securely in the ground beneath 30 tons of concrete and steel rails, ensuring, once and for all, that he could rest in peace.

The museum is open daily May to October from 9:00 a.m. to 5:00 p.m. and the rest of the year Tuesday through

Sunday from 8:00 a.m. to 4:00 p.m. Admission is $2 for adults and $1.50 for seniors and youths ages 6 to 15. (303) 526-0747.

Central City

A nineteenth-century Eldorado, Central City sprang to life in 1859 when gold was discovered in local Gregory Gulch. This mountain wilderness 37 miles west of Denver quickly became a crowded mining camp. Anyone who had been there for three weeks, wrote *New York Tribune* reporter Horace Greeley from the scene, considered himself an old-timer. Along with its neighbors, Black Hawk and Nevadaville, Central City quickly became the state's leading mining center. Instant millionaires hastily constructed Italianate mansions, while new banks sprouted up to tend their money. One of the early moneylenders here was George Pullman, who used his windfall to start the sleeping car company that bore his name.

As the city flourished, it became home of one of the West's great opera houses, attracting famous actors like Edwin Booth and showmen such as Buffalo Bill Cody. A hub of political power, Central City sent two of its favorite sons to the U.S. Senate. Although the rickety Main Street was ravaged by fire in the town's early days, later brick construction proved more durable. While the miners are long gone, today the Central City-Black Hawk historic district enjoys another kind of boom. Tourists come to hear the opera, tour the Lost Gold Mine, or just enjoy walking through the nineteenth-century commercial district. An eclectic mix of Italianate, Territorial, and Gothic Revival architecture, this area features half a dozen restaurants offering live ragtime and Dixieland shows. Central City is also handy to four-wheel-drive trips. An extensive program of cultural activities, including the summer opera season, makes this community a popular destination. In addition, legalized gambling for stakes up to $5 has begun in Central City and neighboring Black Hawk. Casinos with slot machines, blackjack, and poker have been installed in more than a dozen historic downtown buildings such as Central City's Teller House.

Sightseeing Highlights
▲**Black Hawk/the Lace House**—Black Hawk, located
at the junction of Colorado 119 and 279, is a convenient
stop on your way to Central City. This mill town and
freight center had a peak population of about 3,000 during its nineteenth-century mining heyday. A number of
historic buildings are found here, including the Knights
of Pythias headquarters on Selak Street and Fick's Carriage Shop on Main Street. The town highlight is the Lace
House, a carpenter Gothic masterpiece at 161 Main Street.
This 1863 classic features board and batten siding, handsome gable trim, and lots of gingerbread detailing. Now
fully restored, it is open May through September 11:00
a.m. to 5:00 p.m. and by appointment the rest of the year.
(303) 582-5382. If you don't have time for a tour, at least
swing by for a look at this home just one block off your
route to Central City. In Black Hawk, you may want to try
the Black Forest Inn, a popular German restaurant at 260
Gregory Street. (303) 279-2333.
▲**The Teller House/Central City Opera House**—
This historic stone hotel, located at 120 Eureka Street,
hosted celebrities like Ulysses S. Grant and Mark Twain.
The famed Baby Doe, who lived in Black Hawk, periodically occupied a lavish suite here after her marriage to
Senator Horace Tabor. Today visitors can dine or have a
drink at the Face Bar, certainly the best-known saloon in
town. This is the home of the famous Face on the Bar-
room Floor, immortalized in a poem by H. A. D'Arcy. He
tells the story of a promising artist driven to drink when
his beloved Madeline ran off with another man. The face
was painted by a Denver journalist, Herndon Davis. It's
next to the muraled Opera House, where a festival is
staged in July and August. Tours of the Teller House are
offered daily 11:30 a.m. to 4:00 p.m. from May to November. Call for an appointment the rest of the year. Tours are
not offered during opera season in late July and early
August. Opera House tours are offered daily 11:30 a.m. to
4:00 p.m. in May, June, August, and October. During the
rest of the year, tours are available by appointment. For
information on touring both buildings, check at the

Teller House. (303) 582-3200. Admission is $4 for adults, $3 for seniors and children under 12. For advance ticket information on the opera, call (303) 292-6700.

▲▲▲ **Thomas Billings Home**—This 113-year-old Greek Revival at 109 Eureka Street was the home of mercantile store owner Ben Thomas and his wife Marcia. In 1917, the couple moved out of the house, which sat unoccupied until 1987, when it was finally sold by their heirs. Thanks to the dedicated efforts of new owners Mike and Darlene Leslie, this house is now open to the public. What makes this tour one of the best of its kind in the Rockies is the family's possessiveness. None of the furnishings, artwork, toys, clothing, or personal items owned by the Thomases was ever sold. The result is a perfect period house furnished with the original velvet loveseat, cedar chests, fainting couches, and lace curtains. The couple decorated the house with salesmen's samples of nineteenth-century products and advertising art. As a result, you can find posters for Fairy Soap, Durham Tobacco, mouse poisons, and dozens of other products. Salesmen's samples include miniature ice cream makers, washing machines, and a meat grinder. Other one-of-a-kind items include a 1910 Loud Book that triggers a cap gun every time you open it and a Father Christmas paper doll set used to promote the Snappy Shoe Company. Open 9:30 a.m. to 5:00 p.m. daily. (303) 582-3435.

▲▲ **Gilpin County Museum**—Built in 1869 by Cornish stonemasons, this old school building at 228 E. High Street is now one of the state's better small museums. Here you'll find a replica of a miner's Victorian home and a "Temple of Fashion" showing off Victorian gowns, lace coats, and flapper dresses adorned with egret feathers. Nearby are the personal effects of Sheriff Dick Williams, who was gunned down at the Mines Hotel in April 1896. Other highlights include furniture made of dynamite boxes and willow twigs, a diorama of a local mill, a children's collection of miniature dollhouse furniture, and bisque-face dolls. Also exhibited here are a period barber shop, a law office, and a pharmacy. Open daily Memorial Day through Labor Day from 11:00 a.m. to 5:00 p.m. and by appointment the rest of the year. (303) 582-5283.

Other Sights and Attractions

While Central City is the focal point of this historic mining district, it's a good idea to take the short drive up to
the ghost town of **Nevadaville**. A handful of commercial
buildings and a pioneer cemetery are all that remain of
this onetime boomtown of 2,700.

If you have extra time and would like to spend the
night here rather than in Georgetown, try the **Golden
Rose Hotel**, an 1874 stone classic at 102 Main Street.
Rooms here run $50 to $100. (303) 825-1413. The **Gas-
light Inn** at 114 Lawrence Street serves good, moderately
priced German lunch fare. (303) 582-5266.

▲▲ **"Oh My God" Road/Mount Evans**—If you're look-
ing for thrills that top the roller coasters at Elitch Gardens,
give this route a try. Head south out of Central City on
Spring Street to pick up the breathtaking "Oh My God"
Road down Virginia Canyon. This 9-mile graded route to
Idaho Springs offers great views of Chief and Squaw
mountains. (See precautions in Travel Route.) In Idaho
Springs you can take a self-guided tour of the Argo Gold
Mine, open daily 9:00 a.m. to 8:00 p.m. During your visit
you'll see processing equipment, ore cars, and drilling
tools. From Idaho Springs, head west 14 miles on I-70 to
Georgetown.

Itinerary Option: Mount Evans

If time permits today or tomorrow, you'll enjoy the drive
up the world's highest passenger road to the summit of
this Colorado landmark. From Idaho Springs, head west
on I-70 to Colorado 103. This road leads to Echo Lake,
where you'll pick up Colorado 5 to the top of 14,264-foot
Mount Evans. This route (closed in winter) offers a good
overview of both subalpine and alpine terrain. As you
climb above the timberline, you'll want to stop at Summit
Lake to enjoy the great views and take photos for the
folks back home. Near the summit, leave your car at the
parking area and take a short hike to the top of Mount
Evans, where you'll get a great overview of the Rockies
and a number of other 14,000-foot Colorado peaks such

as Long's Peak, Pikes Peak, and Mount Lincoln. It's a good idea to head back to your car in the event of a lightning storm.

Georgetown

This historic community 14 miles west of Idaho Springs has become one of Colorado's most accessible and desirable mountain towns. Settled in 1867, Georgetown came to life with the discovery of silver to become the "Silver Queen of the Rockies." Flush with success, new mining barons built handsome Victorian residences and brick commercial structures.

Today the center of the town looks much as it did in 1893 when the silver market collapsed and the nation switched to the gold standard. A mass exodus ensued, and by the Great Depression this community of 5,900 had dwindled to 300 residents. The Georgetown-Silver Plume National Historic Landmark District is a great place to learn about the history of a silver mining boomtown. A delightful loop railroad, charming hotels, and restaurants make the city an inviting place to stay. In the winter months, the town's proximity to Loveland and Arapahoe Basin ski areas makes it a good place to stay.

Lodging

The **Hardy House** at 605 Brownell Street in Georgetown is a pleasant bed and breakfast offering rooms in the $47 to $72 range. (303) 569-3388. Near exit 228 on the east side of town are the **Georgetown Motor Inn** at 1100 Rose Street, (303) 569-3201, the **Comfort Inn**, (303) 569-3211, and the **Swiss Inn**, (303) 569-2931.

In nearby Silver Plume, the **Brewery Inn** at 246 Main Street also offers bed and breakfast accommodations. (303) 674-5565. Rooms here run $40 to $60. The **Georgetown Resort Service** also rents homes and cabins for a minimum of two nights. Call (303) 569-2665 or write to P.O. Box 247, Georgetown, CO 80444. Reservations are recommended in this community, particularly on weekends and during peak season. If you're camping, try the **Mountain Meadow Campground** located 6 miles

east of Georgetown on US 40. Take exit 232 off Interstate
70. The campground has full facilities. (303) 569-2424.
For more lodging information, call the Georgetown
Chamber of Commerce at (303) 569-2888.

Food
The Ram at 606 6th Street, (303) 569-3263, offers a
wide-ranging menu that includes Italian and Mexican
specialties as well as a popular bar. Italian specialties are
also on the menu at **The Renaissance**, 1025 Rose Street,
Georgetown, (303) 569-3336. For breakfast, try the
Happy Cooker at 412 6th Street, (303) 569-3166.

GEORGETOWN TO LEADVILLE AND ASPEN

Three of the finest mining towns in the Rockies are at the heart of today's agenda, which also includes your first crossing of the Continental Divide via Independence Pass. Along the way you'll go in circles on the Georgetown Loop Railroad, see a fence built out of skis (but is it art?), learn about the tragic love triangle involving a Colorado senator, and enjoy the beautifully restored Jerome Hotel in Aspen.

Suggested Schedule

8:30 a.m.	Walking tour of Georgetown, Hamill House, Hotel De Paris.
10:40 a.m.	Georgetown Loop Railroad.
1:00 p.m.	Arrive Leadville.
6:00 p.m.	Arrive Aspen.

Travel Route: Georgetown to Leadville to Aspen (105 miles)

After visiting Georgetown, take Interstate 70 west to Colorado 91 south to Leadville. Continue south on US 24 to Colorado 82. This narrow road (not suitable for wide trailers or RVs) takes you over 12,095-foot Independence Pass, your highest crossing of the Continental Divide. One of the most scenic mountain drives in Colorado, this route offers a panoramic view of the Sawatch peaks. Open only in the summer and early fall, this shortcut from Leadville to Aspen takes you through a once famous mining region that includes the ghost town of Independence. Farther west, after you pass Lincoln Creek Road, you'll see an unmarked gravel road heading left (south). This is the last spur before you reach Weller campground. Take this side road downhill to a small parking lot. Then head over the footbridge to a trail that continues about 360 feet to a granite outcropping sloping downhill. Walk down to the left about 50 feet to the Roaring Fork River.

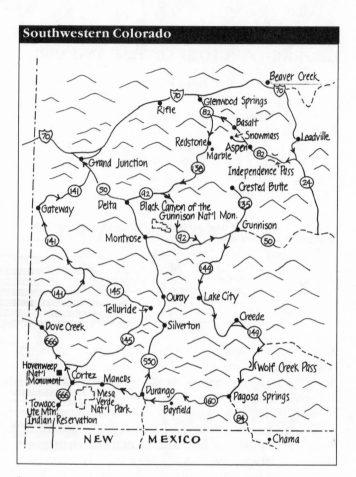

Southwestern Colorado

Here you'll find the Grottoes, beautiful river valley caverns. This is a handsome area to explore. Be sure to use extra caution on the rocks. Then return to Colorado 82 and drive on to Aspen.

Georgetown Walking Tour

Enjoy a leisurely breakfast in Georgetown and then stroll about this historic community. Start your walk on Taos and 9th streets at the Presbyterian Church, a beautiful stone building built in 1874 and restored a century later. Head west toward Clear Creek on 9th Street past Rose

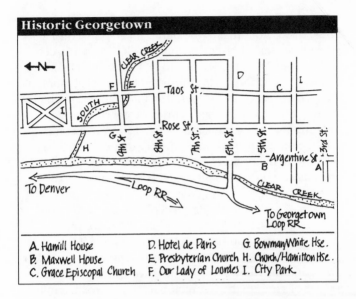

Historic Georgetown

A. Hamill House
B. Maxwell House
C. Grace Episcopal Church
D. Hotel de Paris
E. Presbyterian Church
F. Our Lady of Lourdes
G. Bowman/White Hse.
H. Church/Hamilton Hse.
I. City Park

Street to see the Bowman/White House. Although this 1892 Italianate is not open to the public, you'll be able to see the "coffin door" installed by the family to make room for casket removals after funerals. Continue south down Rose Street, turn right on 7th Street and left on Argentine Street past the old jail to the Hamill House.

This country-style Gothic Revival at 305 Argentine Street was built in 1867 by Joseph Watson, brother-in-law of one of the town's most successful silver mining speculators, William Hamill. A six-year expansion project added a solarium, central heating, and gas lighting. In addition to the home, you can visit Hamill's office building, carriage house, and stable. Highlighted with carpenter's lace, the outdoor privy includes separate stalls for family and servants. The home is open daily Memorial Day through September 30, 10:00 a.m. to 5:00 p.m. During the rest of the year, hours are noon to 4:00 p.m. Wednesday through Sunday. Admission is $3 for adults and $1.50 for seniors. Youths under 12 are admitted free. (303) 569-2840. After leaving the Hamill House, return to 4th Street and turn right three blocks to the Maxwell House, a grand mansion that *Life* magazine calls one of the ten best surviving Victorians in the nation. After passing this home that is not open to the public, head north on Taos Street past Grace Episcopal Church (1867) to 6th Street.

The Hotel De Paris, opened in 1875, was built by Louis Dupuy, a Frenchman who furnished his establishment in the grand manner and attracted an international clientele. Touring today, you can see many nineteenth-century treasures including Haviland china, diamond dust mirrors, a pendulum clock, and tapestry drapes. Meticulously restored, the home is a must for rococo buffs. It's open daily 9:00 a.m. to 5:00 p.m. from Memorial Day though October 1. During the rest of the year, hours are noon to 4:00 p.m. every day except Monday, when it is closed. Admission is $2.50 for adults, $1.50 for seniors, and 50 cents for youths 12 to 16. (303) 569-2311.

After leaving the hotel drive west on 6th Street (toward Clear Creek and the freeway) to Loop Drive and turn left three-fourths of a mile to the Georgetown Loop railroad terminal.

In 1879, an ambitious group of rail builders announced their plan to link two of Colorado's best-known mining camps, Georgetown and Leadville. Standing in the way of their grand plan was Clear Creek Valley, a chasm between Georgetown and Silver Plume 2 miles away. To solve the problem, the Georgetown Breckenridge and Leadville Railway built 4.5 miles of looping track including the 95-foot-high Devil's Gate High Bridge. Although the line never made it to Leadville, the fabulous view from the loop route turned the new line into an instant hit with tourists, who rode the route until 1927. Thanks to local philanthropists, the route was restored and reopened in 1984. Today it is a must ride, offering excursion trips from either the Georgetown or Silver Plume depot. The steam line travels through alpine scenery and makes 14 sharp curves before entering the famous loop. In addition to the one-hour train trip, you can take a one-hour-and-twenty-minute tour of the old Lebanon Silver Mine. Because the temperature inside the mine is 44 degrees, you'll need to bring a coat and walking shoes. At the Silver Plume depot you can also see the engine house and a historic car as well as a gift shop, depot exhibit, and video display. Operated by the Colorado Historical Society, the line offers ten departures daily between 10:00 a.m. and 3:20 p.m. from mid-May through early October. Weekend runs operate in September. Reservations are recommended. Call (303) 670-1686. Fares for the train ride and mine tour are $13.50 for adults and $7.50 for children.

Leadville

The population of Leadville, the highest town in America, soared from 1,200 to 45,000 in early 1879 on the news of major gold and silver strikes. Warmed by bonfires as they worked through that cold winter, miners worked day and night hoping for a lucky strike. While many of the fortunes mined in Leadville were spent on sound investments, others were lost at the gambling tables. Some big winners like Horace Tabor invested in the town, building grand hotels, opera houses, and grand mansions. As the town prospered and emerged as a hub for the Colorado silver and gold boom, Leadville boosters searched for new and better ways to celebrate their success. Perhaps the most spectacular attempt came in 1896. After enjoying a banner year in the mines, the townspeople bought subscriptions to finance construction of the colossal Leadville Ice Palace. This immense Norman ice castle covered three acres. In the center was a large clay-based ice rink, flanked on either side by heated, well-lighted dining rooms, and a dance hall. Although the mining business is long gone and the town's economic mainstay, a molybdenum mine at nearby Climax, has shut down, Leadville is an important center of Colorado gold rush history. It's also a major recreational center offering hiking, jeeping, fishing, and mountain biking opportunities.

Sightseeing Highlights
▲**Healy House and Dexter Cabin**—This Colorado Historical Society site at 912 Harrison Street is a good place to recapture daily life as it was lived during the silver boom of the 1870s and 1880s. This Victorian built by a mining engineer and his wife reflects the elegant life-

style of the period. You're led through by costumed guides. Next door is the Dexter Cabin, a gathering place that served as a poker club for the town gentry. The cabin's modest exterior belies the elegant interior furnishings. This site is open daily from Memorial Day through Labor Day 10:00 a.m. to 4:30 p.m. Tours are available by appointment at other times. Admission is $2.50 for adults and $1.25 for seniors and children ages 6 to 16. (719) 486-0487.

▲ **National Mining Hall of Fame and Museum**—One block south of the Healy House and Dexter Cabin on East 9th Street west of Harrison, this collection housed in an old school building offers a good overview of the mining industry. Displays illustrate mining techniques, showcase iridescent minerals under black light, and honor mining pioneers. Open 9:00 a.m. to 5:00 p.m. daily. Admission is $4 for adults and $2 for children. (719) 486-1229.

▲ **Ski Fence**—Located on 8th Street at Pine, this piece of folk art is a great photo opportunity. A home at this intersection has been fenced with old skis donated by schussboomers. Swing by for a look.

▲ **Tabor Opera House**—Opened in 1879, the Tabor Opera House was the heart of Leadville's cultural life during the boom period. Mining great Horace Tabor's lasting gift to the community, it attracted great stars of the day. While the building needs restoration, it's still fun to explore and see historical displays as well as the square in the floor used by Houdini. Located at Fourth Street and U.S. 24, it's open 9:00 a.m. to 5:30 p.m. every day except Saturday from Memorial Day to October 1. Admission is $3 for adults and $1.50 for children ages 6 to 11. (719) 486-1147.

▲ **Tabor Home and Matchless Mine Cabin**—The home at 116 E. 5th Street and cabin a mile east of town on East 7th Street tell the story of Colorado's most famous mining titan and one-third of a famous nineteenth-century love triangle. You may recall seeing a $7,000 brocade satin wedding dress trimmed in marabou on your Day 1 tour of Denver's Colorado History Museum. It belonged to Elizabeth McCourt Doe, the blond divorcee who took the hand of Senator Horace Tabor (he made it big in politics, too) in one of the nineteenth century's most controversial weddings.

Tabor left his wife, Augusta, to marry the 28-year-old woman in 1883. For years he had kept her as his mistress in the fabulous suite you saw yesterday at the Teller House in Central City. Nicknamed "Baby Doe" by Leadville miners, she was the "other woman" in one of the messier divorce proceedings in Colorado history. Although President Cleveland and many members of Congress attended the Tabor/Baby Doe nuptials, their wives boycotted the ceremony. Afterward, the minister who presided returned his $200 fee, claiming he had been tricked into marrying two divorced people.

Confident that Baby Doe would leave Tabor after his money inevitably ran out, the spurned Augusta prudently invested her $300,000 property settlement. She explained that building up her own fortune and hanging on to her large house would enable her to care for her husband in his old age. Augusta was half right. Horace lost most of his fortune in the Silver Panic of 1893. But Baby Doe stayed by his side as they were reduced to poverty. In 1896, the year after the first Mrs. Tabor died, leaving an estate of $1.5 million, her ex-husband and his second wife were struggling to pay grocery bills. His greatest mine, the Matchless, was abandoned and flooded out.

Finally, in 1898, Tabor was appointed Denver postmaster at $3,500 a year, about what he used to bet in a card game. A year later he took ill with appendicitis. "Never let the Matchless go if I die, Baby," he advised his wife shortly before his passing. "It will make millions again when silver comes back." Baby Doe took his advice and spent the last years of her life in a cabin at the Matchless. She died there in the winter of 1935, trapped by a blizzard. The rescue party found her body frozen on the floor. The Tabor Home and Matchless Mine Cabin are both open daily June 1 to Labor Day from 9:00 a.m. to 5:00 p.m. The Tabor Home is also open the rest of the year Wednesday through Saturday, 9:00 a.m. to 5:00 p.m. Admission to the Tabor Home is $2 for adults and 50

cents for children. (719) 486-0551. Admission to the
Matchless is $2; children 50¢. (719) 486-0371.

Itinerary Option

Leadville, Colorado, and the Southern Railroad offer a
scenic ride on the old Colorado & Southern line. For
information on this glorious route, operated from mid-
June to Labor Day at 9:30 and 2:00 p.m. The same schedule operates weekends during the rest of September. Call
(719) 486-3936. The fare is $16.50 for adults and $9.75 for
children ages 4 to 12.

Aspen

Where do celebrities go when they want to get away from
their public? Where do dudes go when they want to
rough it on a llama trek? Where do real estate developers
sit out on sunny decks and fortify themselves with sushi
as they use their cellular phones to try to close yet
another deal? And where do *2 to 22 Days in the Rockies*
readers get to see all of the above? Aspen, of course. That
cute little mining town adopted by the rich and famous as
their very own hideaway.

In an area originally occupied by the Ute Indians, Aspen
first boomed in 1883 after a major silver strike. Five years
later it was one of the most prosperous cities in the state.
The roughshod mining camp look gave way to handsome
brick buildings, luxurious hotels, and handsome Richardson Romanesque public buildings. The nouveaux riches
celebrated at elaborate balls and built themselves a race-
track out on the edge of town. But in 1893, the country
switched to the gold standard, and the bottom fell out of
the silver market. By the early 1930s, this town of 12,000
had dwindled to a mere 350.

Aspen's salvation came in the 1940s, when Walter
Paepcke created a development company to build a new
ski area and rehabilitate the town's Victorians. While the
skiing business put Aspen back on the map, the city is
now a prosperous year-round resort where movie stars
and their publicists decamp for weeks at a time, VIPs con-
vene at a high-altitude think tank called the Aspen Insti-

tute, and commoners also come to enjoy themselves. The
town takes pride in its drawing power, noting, for example, that Dr. Albert Schweitzer left Africa only once, when
he came to Aspen in 1949 to attend the 200th birthday
celebration of German humanist Goethe. With its gallery
scene, summer music and dance festivals, repertory theater season, and art history museum, Aspen offers plenty
of cultural life. The surrounding mountains offer numerous wilderness opportunities, ranging from day hikes to
week-long backcountry trips. If your idea of a mountain
vacation is a place where you can enjoy prime rib one
night and black linguine the next, you've found the right
historic mining town. Is it any wonder that Jane Fonda,
Jack Nicholson, Don Johnson, Donald Trump, and count-
less other celebrities flock here in the winter months? As
a summer visitor, you'll enjoy all the comforts of Aspen at
a considerable discount. While historic homes here now
sell for $1 million or more, you can enjoy the best of this
mining town without stretching your wallet. As you orient yourself to this community, keep in mind that just
beyond this famous town are some of the most exciting
and accessible treasures in the Rockies.

Lodging

Aspen prices are steep in the winter but drop dramatically during the rest of the year. Prices quoted here reflect
the lower summer season rates.

If you can afford it, the beautifully restored Victorian
Hotel Jerome at 330 E. Main Street downtown is an
excellent choice. Rooms in its more recent addition run
$189 to $409. It's within walking distance of many of the
city's popular attractions. (303) 920-1000. **Aspen Bed
and Breakfast** at 311 W. Main Street offers motel-style
accommodations for $79 to $124 a night. (303) 925-7650.
Alpine Lodge at 1240 E. Highway 82 offers rooms for
$40 to $65 a night. (303) 925-7351. **The Aspen Country
Inn** at 38996 Highway 82 about 3 miles north of town
offers rooms in a 15-acre setting for $72 to $110 a night.
Ask for accommodations on the back side away from the
highway. (303) 925-2700. Dorm accommodations are

available for $20 a night at the **Little Red Ski Haus**, 118
E. Cooper Avenue, (303) 925-3333 (rooms are also available here starting at $50), and at **Snow Queen Lodge** for
$46 to $58 a night. (303) 925-8455. If you're looking for a
condominium near Aspen, try the **Snowmass Resort
Association** at (303) 923-2000, or call the **Aspen
Resort Association** at (303) 925-9000.

All the campgrounds in the Aspen area are very busy in
the summer months. As you drive down Independence
Pass on Highway 82, you'll pass **Lost Man, Lincoln
Gulch, Weller,** and **Difficult** campgrounds. A number
of campgrounds are also located on Maroon Creek Road.
(303) 925-3445. The nearest private campgrounds are 18
miles north on Highway 82 in Basalt. They include the
KOA Campground at 3096 Highway 82, (303)
927-3532, and the **Pan and Fork Trailer Park** at 123
Highway 82, (303) 927-3266.

Food

Family dining in a saloon-style setting is offered at **Little
Annie's**, 517 E. Hyman Street. Try the hamburgers, bar-
becued ribs, or chicken. (303) 925-1098. Arrive early or
be prepared to wait. For inexpensive Mexican food try
Lauretta's of Aspen at Galena and Cooper streets, (303)
925-7464. The setting is unpretentious, the quesadillas
and flautas great. Go for huevos rancheros at breakfast.
The Steak Pit at the corner of Cooper and Original
streets is a good bet for prime rib. (303) 925-3459. The
nude paintings on the wall may not be everyone's idea of
restaurant decor, but the **Mother Lode** at 314 E. Hyman
Avenue is a good bet for pasta, polenta, and other Italian
specialties, as well as beer-battered shrimp. (303)
925-7700. For patio dining at lunchtime, head for **The
Grill on the Park** at 307 S. Mill Street, (303) 920-3700. Try
the hamburgers, sandwiches, or salad Niçoise. For breakfast, head for the **Wienerstube** at 633 E. Hyman Avenue,
(303) 925-3357.

Nightlife

The **Aspen Music Festival**, (303) 925-3254, offers an excellent summer program featuring more than 100 chamber, jazz, choral, and opera performances. Most are staged in the Music Tent; others are held at various venues around town. The **Wheeler Opera House** at 320 E. Hyman Avenue offers plays, films, concerts, and dance performances. (303) 925-2750. **Theater in the Park** offers a summer repertory season from the end of June through mid-September. (303) 925-2750. July through mid-August the **Aspen Summer Dance Festival** performs on Saturday evenings at Aspen High School. If you're in the mood for a cabaret-style show, try the **Crystal Palace Dinner Theater**, 300 E. Hyman Avenue, (303) 925-1455. Another popular spot for dancing is the **Tippler Oyster Bar**, 535 E. Dean Avenue, (303) 925-4977. Author Hunter Thompson has made the **Woody Creek Tavern** semifamous. Take Highway 82 west from town and turn right on Woody Creek Road to 2 Woody Creek Plaza, (303) 923-4585. The **Hotel Jerome Bar** at 330 East Main is also recommended. Although some say fame has turned this venerable hangout into a chic tourist venue, this spot remains the ideal place to toast the Aspen night sky.

DAY 4

ASPEN TO GLENWOOD SPRINGS

Begin your morning with a walking tour of historic
Aspen, seeing some of the city's well-known museums,
Victorians, shops, and parks. You can choose between a
hike, mountain bike trip, or trail ride and then head to
Glenwood Springs for a pleasant rafting trip in the after-
noon. Late in the day there's time for a dip in Glenwood
Hot Springs.

Suggested Schedule

8:30 a.m.	Walking tour of Aspen.
12:00 noon	Maroon Creek Trail.
3:00 p.m.	Colorado River raft trip.
5:00 p.m.	Swim in Glenwood Hot Springs.
Evening	At leisure.

Travel Route: Aspen to Glenwood Springs (53 miles)

Take the walking tour of Aspen, then drive north on Colorado 82 to Maroon Creek Road, turn left, and continue
9 miles to the lake and trailhead. From July 1 to September 15, you'll have to stop after driving about a mile on
Maroon Creek Road, park your car at the designated lot
near Aspen Highlands, and pick up the shuttle bus (to
protect the environment, cars are not permitted) operated by the Forest Service and the Roaring Fork Transit
Agency. Even better, take the Shuttle bus from Aspen's
Rubey Park Transit Center to the Maroon Lake area. After
completing your visit to the Aspen area, head north on
Colorado 82 to Glenwood Springs.

Sightseeing Highlights

Aspen Walking Tour—The Rockies are a very hospita-
ble place, and perhaps no city tries harder to accommodate a wider array of guests than Aspen, from the super
rich to the cross-country bicyclist on a budget. This is a
small town with the kind of amenities you'd expect to

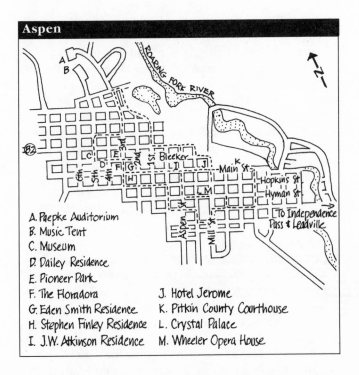

Aspen

A. Paepke Auditorium
B. Music Tent
C. Museum
D. Dailey Residence
E. Pioneer Park
F. The Floradora
G. Eden Smith Residence
H. Stephen Finley Residence
I. J.W. Atkinson Residence

J. Hotel Jerome
K. Pitkin County Courthouse
L. Crystal Palace
M. Wheeler Opera House

find in a much bigger city. I doubt most people come to
the Rockies to eat sushi, but you'll definitely find it here,
flown in fresh daily. Aspen is also the place to see what
movie stars do when they're not on location and catch a
glimpse of controversial local celebrities like the writer
Hunter S. Thompson, who hangs out at the Woody Creek
Tavern. Has success spoiled Aspen? One look at the stag-
gering real estate prices might make you think so. But
there's no charge for Aspen's greatest delight, simply
enjoying the high life. Part of the joy of a visit to Aspen is
walking down the street and listening to people debate
the relative merits of pot stickers, checking out the char-
cuteries, and signing up for your own fast-gaited Tennes-
see walking horse for the day. As the VCR limos cruise
and the Federal Express truck rushes by with the latest
load of imported Oriental rugs and squash blossom art,
you'll be able to check out boutiques with names like

Freudian Slip. No accident, modern Aspen is the kind of place that will make anyone want to rough it.

The perfect spot to begin your exploration is the Renaissance revival **Wheeler Opera House** at Mill and Hyman streets, a monument to Aspen's golden (make that silver) era. Built by Aspen Mine owner J. B. Wheeler in 1889, it is one of the finest venues in the Rockies. Although a fire damaged this stone and brick building in 1912, it has been lovingly restored and now offers a year-round schedule of plays, concerts, dance performances, and films. For information on touring the interior, which is open 10:00 a.m. to 5:00 p.m. Monday through Saturday, call (303) 925-2750. While here, stop by the Aspen Visitor Center to pick up a map of the city to assist you on your walking tour. This route is based on a tour created by the Aspen Historical Society. You can buy a more detailed map and sightseeing guide at their gift shop, in the carriage house behind the headquarters at 620 W. Bleeker Street, (303) 925-3721. After leaving the opera house, walk east down Mill Street toward the river. At East Main Street, turn right to the brick courthouse.

With its silver dome maiden holding the scales of justice, the courthouse is one of the community's finest public buildings. It has been handsomely restored. Continue north on Main to Mill Street and the **Hotel Jerome**. Built of brick and Peachblow sandstone in 1889, this establishment had frescoed walls, marble floors, Eastlake furnishings, and its own greenhouse. An Aspen hub for more than a century, this landmark has been refurbished with paneled transoms, cherrywood doors, cobalt and gold tile, and old mining maps. Sideboards are filled with books, and decanters of sherry on cherrywood tables welcome guests. The eclectic Jerome Bar is now a blend of Eastlake and Anglo-Japanese design.

Continue north to the corner of Aspen and Main to the **J. W. Atkinson Residence (Sardy House)**. Now a bed and breakfast, this 1892 brick home at 128 E. Main Street is on the National Register of Historic Places. Across the street on your left is Paepcke Park, where students frequently play for large audiences during the summer music festival. The park gazebo was built as a bandstand. Continue north past the Eben Smith residence at 338 W. Main Street and the Stephen Finley residence at the corner of Third and Main streets. Turn right on Third to Bleeker Street to **Pioneer Park**. This home, built in 1885, is one of the best-known cottages in town. It was used as a guest house for Albert Schweitzer and his wife when they visited during the Goethe Bicentennial.

If you would like to extend your walking tour after lunch, continue north on Bleeker Street to the **Wheeler Stallard House** at 620 Bleeker Street. This Queen Anne home, built by Jerome Wheeler, serves as headquarters of the Aspen Historical Society. The owner had left his New York business, Macy's Department Store, to restore his health in the clean mountain air. He wound up losing his home following the great silver crash of 1893. The carriage house is an excellent gift shop, offering mementos and publications on the region. The home is open 1:00 p.m. to 4:00 p.m. Tuesday through Sunday from mid-June to late September and December 15 to April 15. The gift shop sometimes has extended hours. Admission is $3 for adults and 50 cents for youths under 14. (303) 925-3721.

▲▲**Maroon Lake**—The Maroon Bells, Aspen's signature mountains above Maroon Creek, are so named because of weathered hematite, an iron-bearing mineral that gives them their red color. Like much of the Rockies, they were created by earthquake faulting and erosion before the glaciers moved in and created this U-shaped valley. Dominated by aspen, blue spruce, and Douglas fir, this region, with its hanging valleys, waterfalls, and creeks, offers excellent hiking opportunities. The shuttle bus from Aspen's Rubey Park Transit Center is recommended in the peak summer season, a fact of life that cuts down on traffic and adds to your enjoyment. It operates from 9:00 a.m. to 4:30 p.m. on the half hour, mid-June to Labor Day. Take the Maroon Creek Trail 2.8 miles to East Maroon Trail and you'll be able to pick up a bus back into town. If you'd like to take a shorter trip, enjoy the 1.1-mile scenic trail that starts at the lake's upper end about a quarter of a mile from the bus stop. Or, if you

have extra time, extend the Maroon Creek Trail into a
6.6-mile trip by continuing to T Lazy 7 Ranch, where the
bus also stops. Keep a sharp eye out for beavers, deer, and
bighorn sheep.

▲▲ **Colorado River Rafting**— You can spend weeks
rafting the Colorado. Today you'll enjoy a taste of the
whitewater experience. Rock Gardens at 1308 County
Road 129 is one of several companies offering short trips
and half-day and full-day excursions. Here's your chance
to raft down Glenwood Canyon, enjoying rapids and a
water fight or two with other vessels. Reservations are
advised. (303) 945-6737.

Aspen Itinerary Options

If you have more time or would like to substitute other
activities during your Aspen visit, here are a few suggestions.

Ashcroft, a ghost town 10 miles west of Aspen on Castle Creek Road, offers a chance to see a handful of historic
mining buildings, join a llama trek, or dine at the expensive, remote Pine Creek Cookhouse. During the winter
months you need a sleigh or cross-country skis to reach
the secluded restaurant. In the summer you can take a 4.5-
hour llama trek from Ashcroft which includes lunch at
Pine Creek. (303) 925-1044.

If you're feeling ambitious, buy a copy of Warren Ohl-
rich's hiking guide, *Aspen/Snowmass Trails*, at the Aspen
Ranger District Office, 806 W. Hallam Street. Highlights
include day hikes such as Difficult Trail and the Hunter
Creek/Smuggler trip. It's easy to rent a bike at Hub of
Aspen, 315 E. Hyman Street, (303) 925-7970. Ride around
town or, if you're in good shape and looking for a chal-
lenge, bike up to Ashcroft (don't forget to allow for the
high altitude). There's a lot of good fishing in this area,
and I'll tell you about one of my favorite spots tomorrow.

Glenwood Springs

One of the biggest mistakes an Aspen visitor can make is
to miss Glenwood Springs. Although less than an hour
north, many visitors fail to take advantage of this town of
5,300. The town's location is perfect, on the Colorado

Aspen Area

River at the foot of Glenwood Canyon. Amtrak provides daily service from Denver over one of the most spectacular rail lines in North America. In the winter, there is moderately priced skiing at Sunlight, and any time of year you can soak in the nation's largest open-air hot springs. The town itself is charming, blessed with nice parks and streams, pleasant Victorians, fine museums, and comfortable inns. Prices here also tend to be lower than in Aspen. And when it comes to rafting, Glenwood is an excellent choice for an hour or a day. Depending on your mood, you can come here for a few hours and return to Aspen for the night or bed down here.

If you only have time for one thermal bath during your tour, be sure to head for **Glenwood Hot Springs** at 401 North River Road. Like the Utes who discovered the curative powers of Yampa Hot Springs (the source of this hot springs pool), modern-day visitors find the waters irresistible. The giant cold pool, complemented by a blazing thermal, is the town's hub. Bring a picnic or sit out on the patio deck and enjoy the scene. A big plus for kids is the water slide. Is it any wonder that Doc Holliday came to Glenwood to recuperate at the hot springs? Much better at gunplay than dentistry (he extracted nearly every tooth from an archenemy while the patient was under laughing gas), he died at age 35, remarking, "This is funny." The hot springs pool is open in the summer from 7:30 a.m. to 10:00 p.m. and 9:00 a.m. to 10:00 p.m. the

rest of the year. During winter months it's closed on the
second Wednesday. Admission is $5.50 for adults and
$3.25 for children. (303) 945-6571.

Lodging

If you want to remain within walking distance of the hot
springs pool, consider the **Hot Springs Lodge** at 401 N.
River Street. (303) 945-6571. Rooms run about $65. The
venerable **Hotel Colorado**, the city's original spa hotel
built in 1893, is also convenient to the water. Rooms at
this establishment, located at 526 Pine Street, run about
$62. (303) 945-6511. Across the street from the train sta-
tion, the **Hotel Denver** at 402 7th Street is in the same
price range. The Club Car Lounge here offers evening
jazz. (303) 945-6565. For bed and breakfast accommodations, try the **Kaiser House** at 932 Cooper Avenue. (303)
945-8827. Rooms run about $60. Budget accommoda-
tions are offered at **Glenwood Springs Hostel**, 1021
Grand Avenue. (303) 945-8545. For camping, try **Rock
Gardens** at 1308 County Road 129. It's two miles east of
Glenwood Springs near Interstate 70 exit 119. (303)
945-6737. This establishment also operates daily rafting
trips. The **Hideout Cabins** at 1293 County Road 117 is
another possibility. Secluded, shaded stream sites are
available, and $50 cabins have kitchenettes. (303)
945-5621. For more information, contact **Central Reservations** in Glenwood Springs at (800) 221-0098 or the
Glenwood Springs Chamber of Commerce at 1102
Grand Avenue, Glenwood Springs, CO 81601, (303) 945-6589.

Food

For Western ambience and moderately priced ribs, steaks,
or seafood, try the **Buffalo Valley Inn** on 3637 Colorado
82, 3 miles south of town. (303) 945-5297. **Sopris Restaurant** on 7215 Colorado 82, 7 miles south of Glenwood Springs, offers more expensive continental cuisine.
(303) 945-7771. On the Roaring Fork River, try
Penelope's at 2525 Grand Avenue. (303) 945-7003. For
steaks, seafood, lamb or duck, a less expensive choice is
the homemade fare at **19th Street Diner** at 1908 Grand
Avenue. (303) 945-9133.

GLENWOOD SPRINGS TO REDSTONE, MARBLE, AND LAKE CITY

Today you leave the Colorado River behind and head down along the Crystal River to one of the finest company towns in the Rockies. After seeing a famous marble quarry and the Black Canyon of the Gunnison, you go on to Lake City, your gateway to the San Juan Range. Along the way you'll have a chance to fish, explore ghost towns, see a splendid castle, and get a fine overview of the high country.

Suggested Schedule

8:30 a.m.	Depart Glenwood Springs.
9:30 a.m.	Arrive Redstone.
12:00 noon	Arrive Marble.
2:00 p.m.	Head over McClure Pass.
6:00 p.m.	Arrive Lake City.

Travel Route: Glenwood Springs to Lake City (215 miles)

Take Colorado 81 south to Carbondale and continue south on Colorado 133 over McClure Pass to Hotchkiss. Pick up Colorado 92 south to Colorado 149 south to Lake City.

Sightseeing Highlights

▲▲▲ **Redstone**—Founded in 1882 by John Cleveland Osgood, founder of the Colorado Fuel and Iron Co., Redstone was designed as a model village. Just before turning left off Highway 133 into Redstone, you'll pass the old beehive ovens where Osgood's company turned high-quality coal into coke that was perfect for steel making. A paternalist eager to improve the sorry image of early western mining camps, he built 84 small homes and cottages, a lodge, a clubhouse, and the village's landmark, the Redstone Inn. With its Dutch tavern design and clock, this hotel is an inviting place to lunch or spend the night.

Another place to spend the night if you want to extend the itinerary here is the Redstone Cliffs Motel, which backs up on the Crystal River, a great fishing stream.

Although coal mining continues in the nearby mountains, most of the town is now in private hands. Brightly painted Victorians with neatly tended gardens line Redstone Boulevard. Backed up against beautiful cliffs, Redstone is a good place to cycle. You can rent a bike here at the Redstone Country Store adjacent to the Redstone Inn. You can also go for a trail ride at the Hitchin' Post located behind this store. During your visit to Redstone you may also want to visit Cleveholm, Osgood's 42-room mansion, which commands nearly a mile of Crystal River frontage. Now called Cleveholm Manor, it offers rooms for $74 to $159. With its mahogany woodwork, velvet dining room walls, and wonderful sun porch, the castle is Colorado's answer to San Simeon. It's at 0058 Redstone Boulevard. (303) 963-3463.

▲▲▲ **Marble**—Ten miles south of Redstone on a spur road east of Colorado 133, this town is best known for an abandoned marble mill. Huge marble fire walls, an old railroad turntable, and, in the warm months, fields of wildflowers are all that remain of this once-flourishing enterprise that supplied the stone for the Tomb of the Unknown Soldier. You can learn about the history of the town and see some old quarry equipment at the Marble Museum, 412 Marble Street. It's open 2:00 p.m. to 4:00 p.m., Memorial Day to Labor Day. After walking about this community of 45, you may want to fish local Beaver Lake. Many visitors also like to take a jeep trip up to the old Yule Marble Quarry, where crews dug out the 600 carloads of stone used to build the Lincoln Memorial. If you have more time, you can also hike the eight-mile round-trip up to the quarry. Other jeep rides can take you to the historic mill at Crystal City, one of the most photographed buildings in the West. For those who have more time, pack trips are also available in the Lead King Basin.

▲▲ **Black Canyon of the Gunnison**—For sheer scenic grandeur, the trip along the north rim of this famed canyon is hard to top. The 53-mile-long Gunnison River chasm, including 12 miles of the gorge inside the monument, plunges as deep as 3,200 feet. One of the few river canyons in Colorado that has not been dammed, the Gunnison offers outstanding fishing, sought out by anglers like former President Jimmy Carter. Although you'll enjoy views of the canyon on today's route, an easy 12-mile side trip from Colorado 92 in Crawford will take you to the north rim ranger station and campground. There's an easy nature trail with great overlooks and wildlife such as hawks and turkey vultures. If you have several days and are in excellent condition, you may want to try one of the difficult trails descending into the canyon. Check first with the ranger before even considering this strenuous trip that requires a day or two of rest before hiking back up. Only experts should attempt this hike, and it is not recommended for children. An easier way to explore the Gunnison Gorge is to drive around the south rim of the canyon via Colorado 92, west from Hotchkiss, US 50 south and Colorado 347 north. Here, several more gradual routes provide access to the Gunnison River. Guided rafting and fishing expeditions depart from Gunnison River Pleasure Park 14 miles east of Delta on Colorado 92. (303) 872-2525.

Lake City

Colorado has many fine mountain communities, and one of my favorites is this little community that offers some of the best recreational opportunities in the Rockies at a fair price. There are two Lake Cities, and this itinerary offers time for you to explore them both. The town itself is a pleasant mountain community that's great fun for western history buffs. It's surrounded on three sides by mountain balconies, carpeted with lush forests pocketed with alpine lakes and laced by streams. Steep trails and roads make this upland region accessible by foot, bike, horseback, or four-wheel-drive vehicles. Whether you choose the strenuous route or simply drive up for a look, you'll quickly fall in love with this high country that offers some of the most spectacular mountain panoramas in the Rockies. And, of course, this area is never crowded.

Founded in 1876, this gold and silver mining town soon attracted miners from all over the world. At its peak, with a population of 5,000, it was the hub of a region that produced more than $10 million worth of silver, gold, copper, lead, and zinc. The nouveaux riches soon built an impressive new residential district with spacious homes decorated with silk wallpaper. While the community was proud of its new schools and impressive residential districts, Lake City also had its share of law and order problems. Best known was Alferd Packer, a guide who left Provo, Utah, on November 21, 1873, with a party of 21 prospectors. In mid-January 1874, six members of this group rejected advice from the local Indians and hiked into the snowy San Juans headed for a camp on the Gunnison River. In mid-April, only Packer resurfaced at an Indian agency, where he asked for a drink of whiskey. The visiting guide soon began playing the part of a high roller, and locals became suspicious when he turned out to have a gun that belonged to one of his companions.

After subsequent investigations, Packer was indicted for the murder of his party on Slumgullion Pass near Lake City. The sensational 1883 trial, filled with charges of cannibalism, ended in a guilty verdict. The Colorado Cannibal won a second trial through a technicality and was sentenced to 40 years at hard labor. In 1901, he was pardoned after an aggressive campaign in his behalf by the *Denver Post*. Today the cafeteria in the student union at the University of Colorado in Boulder is named after him.

By the turn of the century, Lake City's mining business collapsed, and the town became a ranching center. In the 1940s, it was rediscovered by visitors who, together with townspeople, began to restore the community. Although tourism is currently the leading business, the mining industry is hoping to make a comeback. Now Lake City is an excellent place to rediscover the history of this important mining district, explore ghost towns, and enjoy easy access into the San Juans, one of the scenic high points of the Rockies.

Lodging

A primary advantage to Lake City is its informality. While
some dude ranches tend to be pricey and insist on a
week-long stay, Lake City is a flexible place. As long as
you reserve ahead, it's possible to enjoy a dude ranch
experience for a short time at a reasonable price. While
the community offers summer resort amenities ranging
from miniature golf to fishing boat rentals, this town
remains unspoiled. Travel just a few minutes and you can
count on a trail to yourself in splendid isolation. Here you
can enjoy some of the best views in the Rockies, take a
family hike, search for ghost towns, or enjoy geologic
wonders like Sapinero Canyon.

Vickers Ranch, a mile south of town on Colorado
149, offers two-, three-, and four-bedroom cabins ranging from $65 to $140 a night. There's a lake and stream on
the property, jeep and horse rentals, and, on Wednesday
nights, a high country cookout open to those who bring
their own steak. (303) 944-2249. Two miles south of
town on Colorado 149, **Crystal Lodge** offers rooms,
apartments, and cottages for $54 to $85 a night. (303)
944-2201 in summer and (303) 245-3266 in winter. **Lake
View Lodge** on Lake San Cristobal offers cabins, condos,
and lodge rooms in the $29 to $100 range. Boat rentals,
horseback riding, hayrides, and guided fishing trips are
available. There's also a Friday night dinner playhouse.
(303) 944-2401 or (800) 456-0170. **Westwood Resort**
has cabins, some with kitchenettes, from $40 to $55.
(303) 944-2205 in summer and (303) 730-0022 in winter.
Cinnamon Inn, 426 Gunnison Avenue, offers rooms in a
historic 1876 home for $60 to $85. (303) 944-2641.

Camping is available at **Williams Creek Campground**. Take Colorado 149 for 2 miles south of town
and turn right 6 miles to the campground. (303)
641-0471. **Slumgullion Campground** is 6 miles south
of town on Colorado 149. (303) 641-0471. In addition to
these Gunnison National Forest campgrounds, you can
stay at **Woodlake Park**, 2.5 miles south of town on
Colorado 149. (303) 944-2283. Another possibility is
Chick's Trailer and RV Camping at 713 N. Bluff in Lake

City. (303) 944-2287. **Henson Creek R.V. Park**, adjacent
to Henson Creek Bridge, has good fishing access. (303)
944-2394. **Lake View Resort** also has an RV park at Lake
San Cristobal. (303) 944-2401.

Food
The **Lake Fork**, on the east side of Colorado 149 four
miles north of town, offers fine cuisine and an excellent
view. (303) 944-2612. Many visitors enjoy the **Crystal
Lodge** restaurant two miles south of town on Colorado
149. Reservations are advised for this country American
establishment. (303) 944-2201. If you arrive early and
beat the lines, **Lake City Cafe** at Third and Gunnison has
reasonably priced Italian and American food. (303)
944-2733. **Mountain Harvest Restaurant** on Colorado
149 adjacent to Lake City Market is known for its chicken
fried steak, hamburgers, vegetarian dishes, and Sunday
brunch. (303) 944-2332.

LAKE CITY

Today you'll have a chance to go for a trail, jeep, or mountain bike ride, fish some of the streams or mountain lakes, and, of course, explore the historic community of Lake City and learn about Alferd Packer, the man with the legendary appetite. In the evening you might head up the mountain for a community barbecue, play some miniature golf, hit one of the local saloons, or just enjoy a walk in this charming town.

Suggested Schedule

9:00 a.m.	Hit the trail by horse, bike, or jeep.
12:00 noon	Picnic lunch.
Afternoon	Tour historic Lake City, fish, explore, or loaf.
Evening	At leisure.

Touring the Lake City Area

An excellent place to begin a visit to Lake City is the Visitor Information Center on Silver Street downtown, or you can phone the Chamber of Commerce at (303) 944-2527. Here you can pick up maps and information on a variety of ways to tour the region. Directly across the street you can rent mountain bikes and explore the town or bike up Henson Creek past old mining sites. The truly fit can head all the way up Engineer Pass on a very ambitious route. An easier way to make this same trip is to rent a jeep at Rocky Mountain Jeep Rental, (303) 944-2262, and drive up Engineer Pass. The views are great, but use caution on this cliff-hanging route. A detailed map provides all the information you need to visit ghost towns and old mining sites. Of course, you can also enjoy many excellent day hikes. One convenient possibility is to hike along all or part of the four-mile trail to Crystal Lake. The route starts just north of town at the IOOF cemetery. Another possibility is the Williams Creek Trail, which begins at the Williams Creek Forest Service Campground 10 miles above Lake City on Cinnamon Pass Road. The *Lake City Outdoor Journal* is a good resource for touring. A year-long subscription is available by sending $10 to P.O. Box 14, Lake City, CO 81235. Inquire for more information on ordering individual back issues. To find out about other possibilities, pick up the Alpine Explorer Map available at the Visitor Information Center.

Another popular way to explore this area is to take the 9:00 a.m. trail ride that heads up into the high country from Vickers Ranch. Make reservations by calling (303) 944-2249. If you're interested in fishing, consider Big Blue Creek north of town. Follow Colorado 149 11 miles north of town to Alpine Plateau Road. Continue 11 miles on this rugged back road (cars only) to Big Blue Campground. The fishing is great here, and so is the hiking.

The Hinsdale County Museum at 130 Silver Street is a good place to survey Lake City's past. Site of an old hardware store, the building is now a memorial to this mining heyday. Interpretive exhibits cover the town's pioneer days, showcase local artifacts, and, of course, tell the story of Colorado cannibal Al Packer. At the visitor center you can pick up the official guide to the historic homes of Lake City. Among the highlights are the Foote-Vickers Rucker House on Henson Creek, the Beam-Nichols House, and the Youmans-Carey-Starodoj House on Gunnison Avenue. The Frank-Higgins-Thompson House at 430 Silver Street offers a good look at pioneer log cabin construction. Although none of these homes is open to tours, you'll enjoy strolling or hiking around this pleasant mountain neighborhood.

LAKE CITY TO DURANGO

By now you're no stranger to dramatic mountain scenery. But even the most jaded high country traveler will be astonished by today's route through the San Juans. Leaving Lake City, you'll ascend Slumgullion Pass and cross the Continental Divide to the mining town of Creede. After passing near the headwaters of the Rio Grande, you'll crest Wolf Creek Pass. From here it's an easy drive to one of the West's most picturesque mountain towns, Durango, your gateway to the Anasazi Indian culture.

Suggested Schedule

9:00 a.m.	Leave Lake City.
10:00 a.m.	Visit historic Creede Mining District.
12:00 noon	Picnic lunch en route.
3:00 p.m.	Arrive in Durango.
4:00 p.m.	Walking tour of Durango.
Evening	At leisure.

Travel Route: Lake City to Durango (174 miles)
Take Colorado 149 up Slumgullion Pass into the Rio Grande National Forest. After seeing Creede, continue to US 160 and head west over Wolf Creek Pass to Pagosa Springs and Durango. While there are steep and winding sections, the roads are good and traffic is light until you approach the Durango area. As always, use extra caution on the passes.

Sightseeing Highlights
▲ **Slumgullion Pass**—As you leave Lake City, you'll pass the Alferd Packer Historic Site, where the guide's five massacred companions were discovered. It's located near the cutoff to Lake San Cristobal, the state's second-largest natural lake. This popular resort destination was created by a major landslide called the Slumgullion Earthflow. As you begin ascending the pass, you'll see an interpretive display on your left which tells the story of the two huge landslides that caused this major geologic event roughly

350 to 700 years ago. The jumble of rocks prompted
locals to name the slide after a miner's stew. Pause at the
Windy Point Overlook for an overview of the area.

▲▲▲ **Creede**—One of Colorado's last important silver
booms began here on Willow Creek. In true western
fashion, an obscure camp soon turned into a town of
10,000 as new settlers moved in along a two-mile-long
stretch of Willow Creek Canyon. With more than $1 mil-
lion worth of silver shipped out monthly, Creede
boomed until 1893 when the Congressional Silver Act
slashed prices from $1.29 to 50 cents an ounce. Like a
western Sodom, Creede seemed to attract every kind of
lowlife from pool sharks to confidence men to dance hall
girls who minored in pickpocketing. Death hardly ever
took a holiday in the Creede camps, where law and order
types preferred to shoot first and never bothered hanging
around to ask questions afterward. Perhaps the most
famous resident of this community was Jefferson Ran-
dolph "Soapy" Smith. Living by the creed, "Get It While
the Gettin's Good," Smith was a master con man who
used his ill-gotten gains to help finance the construction
of churches, bail out hapless widows and miners, and
even feed homeless dogs. He ultimately moved on to
become one of Denver's first mobsters and then joined
the Klondike gold rush in Alaska, where he was mur-
dered in 1898 at the tender age of 38.

Today this community near the Rio Grande headwaters
attracts trout fishing enthusiasts, hikers, mountain bikers,
and equestrians. There's also a big raft race on the Rio
Grande from Creede to South Fork in June. The focus of
your visit today is the historic Creede Mining District, on
Bulldog Mountain. To explore this area, take Creede Avenue north of town about half a mile and take the right-
hand fork to North Creede. A scenic 7-mile loop drive
takes you through the old mining district, where you'll
see many remnants of the town's heyday. You'll return to
town on West Willow Road. Near the end of your loop
trip, just before driving back into Creede, you'll pass the
ruins of Humphrey's Mill. This cliffside complex offers
great photo opportunities.

Itinerary Option

With advance reservations you can enjoy a tour of the Chimney Rock Archaeological Area. To reach this site, turn south off Highway 160 onto Highway 151, 17 miles west of Pagosa Springs. Continue three miles to the monument gate. During the summer, tours operated daily by the National Forest Service give you a look at the Anasazi settlement located atop this landmark setting. Because you are only allowed to visit the site with a guide, reservations are mandatory. Phone (303) 264-2268 for details on tours offered at 9:00 a.m. daily from mid-May through the middle of September. You may appreciate the fact that tour groups are limited to 30. It is possible to ask for a special tour during the rest of the year if the weather is favorable. Although some of the pueblo ruins here are similar to what you will see at Mesa Verde on Day 9, their setting near the top of this promontory is special. You'll probably be able to see a wide range of wildlife. Also of interest here are special tours of the Southern Ute Indian Reservation located nearby. Call (303) 563-4525 for visitor information. These tours are especially recommended for archaeology buffs with extra time. Rocky Mountain Wildlife Park located five miles south of Pagosa Springs on Route 84 is a good place to see local animals. (303) 264-5546.

Durango

Now that you've seen towns like Central City, Georgetown, Aspen, and Lake City, you've begun to understand why the Rockies are such a perennial favorite with knowledgeable travelers. Today's drive brings you to yet another good reason to visit this mountain region—Durango. If you enjoy small towns as much as I do, you'll give thanks for this community of 13,000. Gateway to Mesa Verde and home base for the nation's premier narrow gauge line, the Durango & Silverton, this Animas River town is also the jump-off point for the 482-mile-long Colorado Trail, which runs from Durango to Denver. From camping to using local helicopters to fly into remote resorts, to hiking, rafting, fishing, and mountain biking, Durango offers a wide range of vacation experiences. This mining town also has an impressive commercial district filled with historical landmarks. In addition, it is the southern end of the Million Dollar Highway, the dramatic US 550 pass that heads north to Silverton and Ouray. Stop by the Durango Area Chamber Resort at 111 S. Camino del Rio for more details. (303) 247-0312.

Lodging

Durango has two beautifully restored hotels, the **Strater** and the **General Palmer**, in the downtown area. The century-old Strater is at 699 Main Avenue. Rates are $62 to $135. (800) 247-4431 or (303) 247-4431. The General Palmer, adjacent to the Rio Grande station, is at 567 Main Avenue. Rates are $75 to $145. (800) 523-3358 outside Colorado, (800) 824-2173 or (303) 247-4747 in Colorado. West of Durango, on the road to Mesa Verde, the **Echo Basin Dude Ranch** offers a moderate weekly rate of $280 to $420. It's at 42688 County Road N, Mancos. (800) 426-1890 or (303) 533-7000. East of town, Wit's End Guest Ranch offers daily rates ranging from $76 to $260. It's at 254 County Road 500, Bayfield. (303) 884-9263. The deluxe Tamarron Resort at 40252 Route 550 North offers resort facilities 16 miles north of town.

The **Iron Horse Inn** at 25926 Highway 550 on the north end of town is another good bet. Suite rooms start around $70. Ask for a room on the railroad tracks and you'll be away from the highway noise. (303) 259-1010. There's also an excellent glass shop, Marigold Glassware, immediately adjacent to the motel. (303) 259-3956. For bed and breakfast, try **Scrubby Oaks** at 1901 Flora Drive. It's set on a 10-acre site overlooking the Animas River. Rooms run from $55 to $65. (303) 247-2176. In the budget category, try the **Durango Hostel International** at 543 E. 2nd Avenue. (303) 247-9905.

For camping, try the **Junction Creek Campground** about 10 minutes from town. Take 25th Street west from North Main Avenue. (303) 247-4874. One mile north of Durango is the **United Campground** at 1322 Animas View Drive. (303) 247-3853. Take US 550, 1.25 miles

north of the Durango city limits. It's located at milepost
25.5. **Lightner Creek Safari Campground** is reached
by taking Colorado 160 3 miles west to Lightner Creek
Road and continuing north 1.5 miles. (303) 247-5406 or
(800) 558-2954. In Silverton, try **Silverton Lakes
Campground** east of town for $12 per night. (303)
387-5721. For additional lodging information, contact
the Durango Area Reservation and Information Service at
(800) 525-8855.

Food
Francisco's at 619 Main Avenue is close to the train station and a convenient place for Mexican food. (303)
247-4098. For pizza, try **Farquarts** at 725 Main Avenue,
(303) 247-5440.

Bar D Chuckwagon Suppers includes western entertainment. Dinner is served at 7:30 p.m. Reserve by calling
(303) 247-5753. Take US 550 6 miles north of town,
drive 1 mile east on Trimble Lane Road, and then 1.5 miles
north on Colorado 250. Open Memorial Day through
Labor Day. For seafood, try the **Red Snapper**, 144 E. 9th
Street. (303) 259-3417.

To enjoy the Strater Hotel at 699 Main Avenue, try
Henry's Victorian dining room. (303) 247-4431. For
steak, dine at the **Ore House** at 147 Sixth Street, (303)
247-5707.

Durango Walking Tour
Take time to orient yourself to this historic community. A
convenient starting point is the Denver and Rio Grande
Depot at the foot of Main Avenue. If you're taking the
train excursion tomorrow, stop by the office and pick up
your tickets. Then head north along Main to visit the
General Palmer and the Strater, two of the state's finest
historic hotels. Continue past the vintage downtown
office blocks to 11th Street, where you turn right, go to
3rd Avenue and then turn left. Here you'll get a good
overview of the city's historic residential district, ranging
from the mansions of mining kings to the simple homes
of the working class. The limestone-faced Presbyterian

Church at 3rd Avenue and 12th Street is across the street
from one of the city's fine Queen Annes, the Wilson Per-
kins House. Next door is the Amy House, a fine Victorian
with a large cupola. To learn more about Durango's past,
visit the Animas Museum at 3065 West 2nd Avenue. Open
10:00 a.m. to 6:00 p.m. Monday through Friday and 11:00
a.m. to 4:00 p.m. Saturday and Sunday from Memorial
Day through Labor Day. (303) 259-2402. You can shop
here for a wide range of Indian arts and crafts at the Toh-
Atin Indian Art Gallery, 145 W. 9th Street, (303) 247-8277.
In the summer months, you can also enjoy melodrama at
Diamond Circle Theater in the Strater Hotel, 699 Main
Avenue. (303) 247-4413.

Helpful Hint

Durango/Purgatory Handicapped Sports Association is a
complete referral program. Write to P.O. Box 1884,
Durango, CO 81302, or call (303) 259-0374.

DURANGO TO SILVERTON

Today you'll enjoy one of the nation's finest steam excursion trips, from Durango along the Animas River to Silverton. After exploring Silverton you'll return to Durango in time for dinner. Or, if you prefer, take a spin on the Million Dollar Highway to Silverton, Ouray, and Telluride.

Suggested Schedule

8:30 a.m.	Board the Durango to Silverton Narrow Gauge.
11:45 a.m.	Arrive Silverton.
2:00 p.m.	Leave Silverton.
5:15 p.m.	Arrive Durango.

Sightseeing Highlights
▲▲▲ **Durango to Silverton Narrow Gauge**—If you've planned ahead and made reservations, you can count on enjoying one of America's great rail adventures. If you haven't, it still may be possible to get tickets for this popular trip that has been operating on this line since 1881. The 45-mile narrow-gauge route from Durango to Silverton is served by coal-fired, steam-operated locomotives. You can choose between fully enclosed coaches or open-air gondolas. Either way, you'll enjoy this trip that provides direct service to the wilderness for backpackers, fishermen, and hikers who disembark at the Needleton and Elk Park flag stops. The train also makes occasional stops to pick up or unload freight. With most of the trackage cutting through San Juan National Forest wilderness, the ride is a real cliff-hanger.

Originally built to haul out gold and silver from the San Juan Mountains, your train is powered by vintage steam equipment. If you can't get a seat on the full-day trip to Silverton, you may be able to take one of the half-day trips on the sister line, the Animas River Railway. This motorized train runs from Rockwood, 17 miles north of

Durango, to Elk Park. You can also buy a ticket that allows an overnight layover in Silverton. You can stay in Silverton as long as you'd like before returning to Durango. Train fares run $37.15 for adults and $18.65 for children ages 5 through 11. Parlor car tickets are $63.85. You can make reservations by calling (303) 247-2733. The station is at 479 Main Avenue. Be sure to pick up your tickets the night before departure. Doris Osterwald's guide *Cinders and Smoke* is a helpful mile-by-mile companion to your trip. It's available at the depot gift shop.

▲▲▲ **Silverton**—More than a century ago, the railroad put Silverton on the map. The townspeople waited for over two years as crews blasted their way through Animas Canyon to build the railbed. The train's arrival in 1881 provided a direct link to Durango and the outside world. It instantly made Silverton the center of the once isolated San Juan mining district. Today the railroad remains a local economic mainstay, bringing in tourists by the thousands each week.

After lunching at the picnic tables near the train station, or at the Bent Elbow where a piano player performs at lunch, you'll have time to enjoy Silverton. Go directly to the San Juan County Jail on Greene Street near 15th Street to visit the county museum. (303) 387-5838. From here, walk down Greene to 13th, where you can visit the *Silverton Standard and the Miner*, a historic office that is home to the local newspaper. Next door is the Grand Imperial, an old railway hotel. Across the street is the Teller House, a onetime boarding house that continues to offer inexpensive lodging. On the ground floor is the French Bakery restaurant. Continue down Greene Street to see the old livery and the miner's union hall. After you've had a chance to leisurely explore the town and do some shopping, make your way back to the depot for the return trip to Durango.

If you want to spend the night here, try the **Alma House Bed & Breakfast** for $40 to $60. It's at 220 E. 10th Street. Open May 15 to September 25. (303) 387-5336. Off-season, call (303) 259-2884.

Itinerary Option: Million Dollar Highway

One of the finest drives in Colorado heads north via US 550 from Durango. Built through the mountains at the once stupendous cost of $1 million a mile, this route parallels the train tracks for 17 miles to Rockwood, then continues over Molas Divide to Silverton. From here you can continue over Red Mountain Pass to historic Ouray and then head west at Ridgway on Colorado 62 west and Colorado 145 east to Telluride, where you may be tempted to explore and spend the night. From this point you can continue south on Colorado 145 to Colorado 184 to Mancos. Pick up US 160 west to Mesa Verde National Park. Of course, you can also double back from Telluride through Ouray and Silverton if you'd prefer to spend another night in Durango. The Million Dollar Highway is one of the scenic high points of Colorado and offers a good look at some of the most memorable countryside in the San Juans. The 59-mile section from Durango to Silverton is steep, winding, and gorgeous. Grand waterfalls, sheer cliffs, and 12,200-foot-high Red Mountain Pass are just a few of the highlights. The descent into Ouray is the most spectacular piece of paved road in Colorado.

MESA VERDE

Of the four national parks on your 22-day itinerary, only
one is dedicated to the works of man. The cliff dwellings
of Mesa Verde have fascinated visitors to Colorado since
they were discovered more than a century ago. A visit
here raises almost as many questions as it answers. How
did the Anasazi Indians build these lofty homes? Why did
they want to live in these remote perches? What did they
do with people who had a fear of heights? And why did
the Anasazi disappear? You'll get some of the answers to
these questions today.

Suggested Schedule

7:00 a.m.	Leave Durango.
9:00 a.m.	Visit Cliff Palace.
10:30 a.m.	Visit Balcony House.
12:00 noon	Lunch.
1:00 p.m.	Visit Spruce Tree House.
2:30 p.m.	Mesa Verde Museum.
3:30 p.m.	Mesa Top Ruins.

Overnight at Mesa Verde.

Travel Route: Durango to Mesa Verde (67 miles)
From Durango, take US 160 west past Mancos to the Mesa
Verde entrance and drive south into the park.

Mesa Verde
Mesa Verde is a high green plateau with dramatic canyons.
Abandoned more than six centuries ago by the Anasazi
Indians, these cliff dwellings and mesa-top ruins remained
untouched until cattle ranchers found them in 1888.
Although the mesa was first seen by Anglo-Americans
in 1859, the region was first explored in 1874 by photog-
rapher William H. Jackson, who published pictures of the
Mancos River Valley cliff dwelling ruins. In 1887, local
rancher Al Wetherill spotted the biggest of the ruins, the
Cliff Palace. A year later, his brother, Richard, and a
brother-in-law, Charlie Mason, visited Cliff Palace and

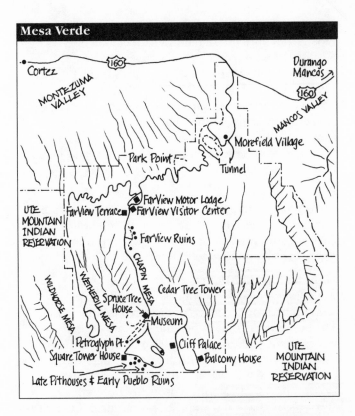

several other major dwellings. Their discovery of the stonemasoned cities on the canyon walls soon attracted archaeologists from America and abroad, and in 1906, Congress acquired the site from the Ute Indians. Today the park is a World Heritage Site and the most visited of the southwestern Colorado/southeastern Utah Anasazi sites, which also include Hovenweep National Monument, Lowry Ruins, and the neighboring Ute Mountain Tribal Park. For general park information, call (303) 529-4475.

Lodging

Far View Lodge, a national park facility on the mesa, offers rooms for $69 to $80. Reservations are mandatory for these modern units, which, as the name suggests,

offer great panoramas of the surrounding countryside.
Open from April through mid-October. Call (303)
529-4421 for reservations. Or write to P.O. Box 277,
Mancos, CO 81328. In the winter, call (303) 533-7731 for
information.

You can camp 4 miles from the park entrance at
Morefield Campground. This is the only campground
at Mesa Verde, and it operates on an unreserved basis.
Early check-in is recommended. Summer events begin
here at 9:00 p.m.

Food

There's a restaurant and cafeteria at Far View and addi-
tional food service at Spruce Tree and Wetherill Mesa.
Groceries are available at Morefield Campground, Far
View Terrace, and Spruce Tree Terrace.

Sightseeing Highlights

▲▲▲Park Point—On your ascent of the mesa, you'll
see a number of fine views of the surrounding region.
The best is Park Point. When the skies are clear, as they
typically are, you can enjoy a 100-mile view of the Four
Corners region. To the north are Utah's Abajo and Manti-
La Sal mountains as well as Colorado's Lone Cone,
Dolores Peaks, and Mount Wilson. To the south are New
Mexico's Hogback and Shiprock promontories as well as
Arizona's Lukachukai Mountains and Carrizo Mountains.
In a westerly direction are Colorado's Sleeping Ute Moun-
tain and Montezuma Valley. In the east are Colorado's La
Plata and Mefee Mountain and the Mancos Valley.

▲▲▲Cliff Palace—The largest cliff dwelling in North
America is easily explored via a self-guiding trail. The
Anasazi first settled this region in the sixth century. At
first they lived in pithouse villages built on top of the
mesa. But by A.D. 1200 they had progressed from these
pole and adobe dwellings to their cliffside homes. Like
the cowboys who first discovered this sandstone alcove,
you'll be astonished by the breadth of this 217-room
dwelling pocketed by 23 kivas or ceremonial rooms. Built
primarily of sandstone, the palace was the ultimate Native
American condo where the Indians lived, worked, wor-

shiped, and buried their dead. As families grew, the Anasazi added space by knocking out walls and doorways and building new rooms. Superb masons, the Indians built sturdy dwellings. Unfortunately, as the blackened interior walls attest, ventilation was poor in their smoky quarters. Of special interest are the kivas or ceremonial chambers, where the Indians prayed for rain, a good growing season, or luck in hunting. They were also used as gathering places, and weaving was done there. In the bottom is the *sipapu*, the symbolic entrance to the underworld.

▲▲▲**Balcony House**—Located 600 feet above Soda Canyon, Balcony House is another excellent example of the Anasazi's superb masonry technique. Secure from enemies, about 50 Anasazi lived in this 35- to 40-room complex. You enter the house by climbing a 32-foot ladder on the north side of the dwelling. Entering the north courtyard, you'll see the first balcony, where residents enjoyed a good overview of the region. While archaeologists believe this location was an excellent defensive structure, there is no evidence that the Anasazi were ever attacked. They may have simply been worried about potential enemies or trying to safeguard their food from one another. This remote location also protected many notable Indian artifacts, including an extraordinary medicine man's cache uncovered in the 1950s. It was filled with turquoise, shell beads, and disk pendants. Your guided tour of the site includes crawling through a small tunnel used by the Anasazi and climbing steep steps and ladders required to exit. You may have to wait your turn to visit this site, which is not recommended for people with mobility problems or a fear of heights.

▲▲▲**Spruce Tree House**—A picturesque trail leads down through a piñon forest to this 114-room dwelling that was home to about 150 Anasazi. At the center of community activity were the large courtyards. Here the Indians ground corn, made pottery and baskets, prepared meals, and made tools or blankets. Adjacent to the roofless kiva are three tiers of rooms and a large trash disposal area that has been a gold mine for archaeologists. Use the ladder to descend into the kiva at stop 5. Although experts have shored up and rebuilt small portions of the Spruce Tree House, this 700- to 800-year-old structure is a credit to its contractors. About 95 percent of the site is unreconstructed.

▲▲▲ **Chapin Mesa Archaeological Museum**—In this museum you can put together many of the pieces of the Mesa Verde story. You'll learn about the development of pueblo architecture and pottery, clothing, hunting, and farming techniques and see exhibits on pottery, weaving, and beadwork. The discovery of Mesa Verde, preservation techniques, and other Anasazi ruins and points of interest in southwestern Colorado are also covered. The bookstore is excellent. Additional interpretive information can be found at the Far View Visitor Center adjacent to Far View Terrace. Open 8:00 a.m. to 6:30 p.m. May through October and 8:00 a.m. to 5:00 p.m. the rest of the year. Evening talks are also offered at 9:00 p.m. at the Morefield Campground.

▲▲▲ **Mesa Top Ruins**—For an overview of 600 years of Anasazi heritage, turn right at the first intersection after leaving the museum parking lot, to Ruins Road Drive. This easy loop, the Mesa Top Drive, takes you to Square Tower house, pithouses, pueblo ruins, and the Sun Point overlook. The Mesa Top Drive gives you a panoramic look at the architectural evolution of this area beginning with the Modified Basket Maker period around A.D. 600 and culminating with the famous pueblo cliff dwellings you've just seen. Although the Indians first came to the region about 2,000 years ago, it was another six centuries before they built their first permanent homes on the mesa. The early houses were pits covered with poles, sticks, branches, and mud. Gradually the pits became deeper and larger and were reinforced with sandstone slabs. Shafts were added to help ventilation. By A.D. 850, the Indians began living in post and adobe surface dwellings known as pueblos, and a century later they began clustering together in larger villages. All these construction techniques eventually contributed to the first cliff dwellings, which began to appear on the mesa around the eleventh century.

Itinerary Option

If you'd like to go back to this region's roots and leave the park masses behind, consider extending your trip with a visit to Ute Mountain Tribal Park, which offers one of the finest Indian-led tours in the Rockies. Day hikes, tours, overnight camping, and backpacking are all available on this fascinating Indian reservation located south of Mesa Verde. Here's how to visit this little-known site that's well worth your time. First, make a reservation by calling (303) 565-3751, ext. 282, or writing to the park at Towaoc, CO 81334. From Mesa Verde, it takes about two hours to reach the reservation headquarters. Begin by returning to US 160. At Cortez, the highway swings south to Towaoc, where you'll meet your guide. This 125,000-acre site contains more than 2,000 cliff dwellings, including some that compare favorably with the best of Mesa Verde. There are no hotels, restaurants, bars, or slide shows in this primitive park. But the tours are sensational. Unlike Mesa Verde, where access is very restricted, you can climb (and possibly even spend the night at) Eagles Nest Ruin, see buried artifacts uncovered where they were discovered, and have a chance to explore ruins seen by only a handful of white men. Prices are very reasonable. Half- and full-day trips run as little as $30 to $50. Guided backpacking trips are also reasonable. "I think the tribe has done a very nice job developing their ruins," says Mesa Verde's superintendent. "Clearly, they have learned from some of the mistakes we have made."

For a chance to see a working archaeological site and try the Anasazi life-style, visit the Crow Canyon Archaeological Center at 23390 County Road K., Cortez. (303) 565-8975. This seminar, offered Tuesday, Wednesday, and Thursday from late May to mid-October, includes lunch.

Helpful Hint

If you have extra time and would like extend your trip to adjacent areas of New Mexico, Arizona, and Utah, try Richard Harris's *2 to 22 Days in the American Southwest* (Santa Fe: John Muir Publications, 1993). You can pick up his itinerary on Day 5 and sample as much of this region as you care to before returning to the Rockies.

MESA VERDE TO GRAND JUNCTION

Today's drive leads through a remote red rock canyon to
Grand Junction and the Colorado National Monument.
This beautiful backcountry route includes a stop at a
superb Anasazi Indian museum, a cutaway view of geologic history along the scenic Dolores River, and a chance
to hike along a majestic Colorado River gorge.

Suggested Schedule

8:00 a.m.	Leave Mesa Verde.
9:30 a.m.	Visit Anasazi Heritage Center in Dolores.
11:00 a.m.	Drive through Dolores Canyon.
3:00 p.m.	Explore Colorado National Monument.
6:00 p.m.	Check into your room or campground.

Travel Route: Mesa Verde to Grand Junction (272 miles)

This scenic drive is a relaxed, somewhat winding trip
with light traffic. Leave Mesa Verde National Park on US
160 westbound to Colorado 145, which takes you north
to Colorado 184 westbound. After visiting the Anasazi
Heritage Center, continue west on Colorado 184 to US
666. Turn north and pass through Dove Creek to
Colorado 141. Take this highway north through Dolores
Canyon to US 50. Continue northwest to Grand Junction.
US 50 becomes 5th Street. Take it to Grand and turn left.
Cross the Colorado River to Monument Road and turn
left. After completing the 23-mile drive through
Colorado National Monument, exit the west entrance to
Fruita. Turn right on Broadway to Grand Junction.

Sightseeing Highlights

▲▲ **Anasazi Heritage Center** — This museum, located
three miles southwest of Dolores, at 27501 Colorado 184,
is home to more than two million Indian artifacts, shards,
ruins, pottery, and baskets that belonged to the Indians

between the time of Jesus and A.D. 1300. Many of the best
are now on display thanks to the hard work of scientists
who excavated the site of the nearby Dolores River Recla-
mation Project. In addition to Anasazi artifacts, you'll find
exhibits on Indian life, a pithouse replica, and discovery
areas where visitors can handle Native American treasures
or grind corn. Also on display are farming and craft
exhibits. Adjacent to the center are the twelfth-century
Anasazi ruins of Dominguez and Escalante. Both can be
toured via self-guided walks. Open daily 9:00 a.m. to
5:00 p.m. (303) 882-4811.

Itinerary Options: Hovenweep National Monument and Lowry Ruins

If you're hooked on the Anasazi story, here are two excellent side trips that will add to your understanding and
enjoyment of this region. Both lack the crowds that
sometimes descend on Mesa Verde's best-known cliff
dwellings. Hovenweep is reached by taking US 160 south
from Cortez 3 miles and then continuing west 39 miles
via McElmo Canyon Road, which is dirt (access may be
restricted after rainstorms). Spanning the Utah/Colorado
border, this monument offers a chance to visit half a
dozen ruins, including the imposing Square Tower built
to defend ancient springs. You'll have to hike to see the
other oval and circular towers such as Cutthroat Castle

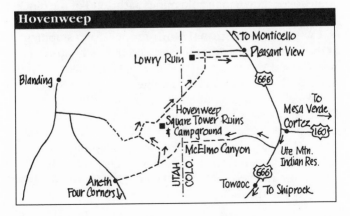

and Hackberry Canyon, a journey that is especially
rewarding at sunset. There's a campground near Square
Tower. The park is open 9:00 a.m. to 5:00 p.m. More
information is available at Mesa Verde National Park.
(303) 529-4461.

From Hovenweep you can drive northeast 25 miles on
the unpaved Pleasant View Road to the cutoff for Lowry
Pueblo, built by the Anasazi in the late eleventh century.
This National Historic Landmark has one of the largest
known kivas, a ceremonial room adorned with beautifully preserved murals. From Lowry drive 9 miles to US
666 and rejoin the main route. Be sure to check the
weather forecast before visiting these two monuments in
the fall, winter, or spring, as sudden snowstorms can
make access difficult.

One of the scenic highlights of any Colorado visit,
Dolores Canyon is backroad driving at its finest. This ura-
nium mining country reached by Colorado 141 includes
appropriately named villages like Nucla and Uravan. The
latter is the gateway to this red rock sandstone canyon on
the Dolores River. Beautifully sculpted by the elements,
this multicolored canyon is the backdrop to a memorable
drive through Dakota, Wingate, and slickrock Entrada
sandstone as well as red and gray shale. Eight miles north
of Uravan you'll pass Hanging Flume, the cliffside
wooden channel that carried water along a 6-mile canyon
route to local hydraulic gold mines at the end of the nineteenth century.

▲▲▲ **Colorado National Monument**—After stopping
at the visitor center near the west end of this 1,000-foot-
deep Grand Valley canyon, enjoy a short hike like the one
to Coke Ovens. You can take a longer hike down No
Thoroughfare Canyon or enjoy the 23-mile Rim Rock
Drive. Short hikes to overlooks are available all along the
drive, or hikers can take longer trails down to the canyon
floor. The visitor center is open daily from June 1 to
Labor Day from 8:00 a.m. to 8:00 p.m. The rest of the
year hours are 8:00 a.m. to 4:30 p.m. daily. Closed Christmas Day. (303) 858-3617.

Grand Junction

The largest city in western Colorado, Grand Junction is located at the confluence of the Colorado and Gunnison rivers. This region of 85,000 is the heart of a major fruit-growing district and gateway to popular destinations like Utah's Canyonlands. If you have extra time, you may want to visit the **Museum of Western Colorado** at 4th and Ute avenues, (303) 242-0971, to learn about the area's natural, political, and cultural heritage. It's open 10:00 a.m. to 4:45 p.m. Memorial Day through Labor Day, Tuesday through Saturday. During the rest of the year, hours are 10:00 a.m. to 4:45 p.m. Tuesday through Saturday. **Dinosaur Valley Museum** at 4th and Main streets offers a look at local paleontology in this fossil-rich region as well as half-size animated dinosaurs. (303) 243-3466. Also of special interest is the **Cross Orchards Living History Farm** at 3079 F Road, where you'll see interpretive exhibits that bring to life this region's agrarian heritage. (303) 434-9814. It's open mid-May to November 1, from Wednesday to Saturday 10:00 a.m. to 4:00 p.m. Mountain bikers may want to try the 128-mile Kokopelli Trail to Moab, Utah, in the late spring or early fall.

Lodging

Cider House Bed and Breakfast has rooms for $38 to $42. It's at 1126 Grand Avenue. (303) 242-9087. The **Best Western Horizon** at 754 Horizon Drive runs $30 to $60. (303) 245-1410. The **Gate House** is a comfortable bed and breakfast at 2502 N. 1st Street. (303) 242-6105. Rooms run about $30 to $58. This structure, built as part of the **Osgood Mansion** (now the Cleveholm Manor) in Redstone, was moved to Grand Junction in 1945. Camping is available for $6 at the **Colorado National Monument** year-round (see Sightseeing Highlights). The campground has tables, fireplaces, and rest rooms. In addition, you can camp near the monument at **Fruita Junction RV Park**. It's located at 607 Highway 340, Fruita. (303) 858-3155. Full hookups are available. Units run $10 to $12. For more lodging ideas, call the Grand Junction Chamber of Commerce at (800) 962-2547.

Food

For steak or prime rib, try **The Winery** at 642 Main Street. (303) 242-4100. **GB Gladstones** at 2531 North 12th Street is another upscale possibility offering steaks, seafood, and pasta. (303) 241-6000. **Sweetwater's** is a good choice for northern Italian patio dining on a warm night. It's at 336 Main Street. (303) 243-3900. Another moderate Italian possibility is **Pantuso** at 2782 Cross-roads Boulevard. (303) 243-0000. Modestly priced Mexican fare is available at **Los Reyes**, 811 S. 7th Avenue. (303) 245-8392.

DINOSAUR NATIONAL MONUMENT AND FLAMING GORGE

Dinosaur National Monument, a dramatic drive through the Uinta Mountains, and a visit to the Flaming Gorge National Recreation Area are the highlights of today's journey as you make the transition from Colorado to Wyoming via Utah. You'll have a chance to see dinosaur fossils and view Indian petroglyphs, wildlife, and one of the West's most picturesque red rock canyons.

Suggested Schedule

7:30 a.m.	Leave Grand Junction.
10:30 a.m.	Arrive at Dinosaur National Monument.
12:00 noon	Picnic lunch at Dinosaur National Monument.
2:30 p.m.	Depart for Vernal and Uinta Mountains.
4:30 p.m.	Visit Flaming Gorge National Recreation Area.
6:00 p.m.	Overnight in Green River, Wyoming.

Travel Route: Grand Junction to Green River (254 miles)

Take I-70 west 17 miles to Colorado 139 and head north to Rangely. Head west on Colorado 64 another 18 miles to Dinosaur. Continue west on US 40 21 miles to Jensen, Utah. Here you'll pick up Utah 149 for the 7-mile trip to Dinosaur National Monument. After visiting here, return to US 40 where you drive west 13 miles to Vernal. Hold on to your hat as you spiral north on US 191 for 35 miles into the Uinta Mountains. When you reach US 44, turn left and drive 31 miles to Manila. Here you'll pick up Wyoming 530 north along the beautiful Flaming Gorge Reservoir for the final 45 miles into Green River. With the exception of the drive through the Uinta Mountains, most of this trip is easy going. Traffic should be light except in the vicinity of Flaming Gorge, where you can expect more company.

Sightseeing Highlights ✓

▲▲▲**Dinosaur National Monument**—Spanning the
Colorado/Utah border, this 325-square-mile park is distinguished by both its paleontological treasures and its
geologic features. The place to begin a visit is the Dinosaur Quarry 7 miles north of Jensen, Utah. Here in the
quarry you'll see the experts chip away at sandstone to
expose the bones of Diplodocus, Stegosaurus, Allosaurus,
and other dinosaurs. Over 2,300 fossilized bones are on
display in the quarry, and you can get a good overview of
this former dinosaur stomping ground. Partial skeletons
of ten dinosaur species that once lived in this region can
be seen on the 200-foot quarry face. Dinosaur National
Monument's Dinosaur Quarry is open from 8:00 a.m. to
4:30 p.m. daily June through August and the same hours
Monday through Friday the rest of the year. For more
information, call (801) 789-2115.

After finishing your orientation, enjoy this 22-mile-
long driving tour. The route (pick up a self-guiding tour
brochure at the visitor center) offers a good overview of
the monument sculpted by two great rivers, the Green
and the Yampa. Your route leads past Split Mountain, a
promontory divided in half by the Green to produce a
beautiful canyon. Along the way you'll see Cub Creek Valley, multicolored hills, old ranches, and Elephant Toes
Butte, and you'll climb up a small hill to examine petroglyphs made by the Fremont Indians more than nine centuries ago. At the end of the drive is the Josie Morris
Cabin, a memorial to a woman who homesteaded here
without modern conveniences until 1964. Easy hikes take
you up Box or Hog Canyon. Either of two campgrounds
on this route, Green River or Split Mountain, is convenient for lunch.

It's easy to extend your visit to Dinosaur Quarry with a
longer hike or rafting tour. At the Quarry Visitor Center
you can get self-guiding tour information on several
popular trips. Harpers Corner Trail, which begins at the
end of Harpers Corner Road, is a pleasant 2-mile hike
through piñon-spruce woodland. Another excellent
choice is the 8-mile-long round-trip Jones Hole trail that

leads from the Jones Fish Hatchery through a narrow canyon to the Green River. Check with the park rangers for weather information before hitting the trail. Bring your own drinking water. Another popular way to explore Dinosaur National Monument is to take a one- to five-day raft trip on the Green or Yampa River. These excursions are operated from late spring through early fall. For more information, check with the visitor center or call Don Hatch River Expeditions, (801) 789-4316. To extend your stay, visit the Colorado headquarters of Dinosaur National Monument at Harpers Corner Road and US 40, two miles east of Dinosaur. (303) 374-2216.

▲ **Utah Field House of Natural History**—Located at 235 E. Main Street in Vernal, this museum features interpretive dinosaur displays, mineral exhibits, and Native American history. Adjacent to the museum are fourteen life-size dinosaur exhibits in a garden setting. In the museum complex, the visitor center provides brochures on nine self-guided tours of the Vernal region. Of special interest for today's itinerary are Tours 2 and 7, which lead north to the Flaming Gorge National Recreation Area. Open daily from 8:00 a.m. to 7:00 p.m. June through August. The rest of the year hours are 9:00 a.m. to 5:00 p.m. (801) 789-3799.

▲▲▲ **Flaming Gorge National Recreation Area**— You've seen a lot of pretty country on your trip through the Rockies, and this afternoon our itinerary takes you to one of the most overlooked gems in the Rockies. Because it's a bit off the beaten track, many interstate travelers unfortunately sail right by this southern Wyoming highlight. From Vernal you'll head north into the Uinta Mountains high country. Keep a sharp eye out as you enter this area and you'll probably spot deer and possibly antelope, moose, and bighorn sheep. After leaving US 191 for Utah 44 west, turn off to Red Canyon Overlook for a fine view of the Flaming Gorge region, one of the scenic highlights of your trip. Here, 1,300 feet above this gorge cut out of the Uintas by the Green River, is a good view of this vast lake known for its trout and salmon fishing. A visitor center here provides general information on the gorge area.

It's open daily 9:30 a.m. to 5:00 p.m. Memorial Day
through Labor Day. (801) 889-3713. From here your route
proceeds along the southern and western rim of the
reservoir to Green River, Wyoming.

Lodging

In Green River, the **Coachman Inn Motel** at 470 E.
Flaming Gorge Way, (307) 875-3681, and the **Super 8
Motel** at 280 W. Flaming Gorge Way, (307) 875-9530,
both offer rooms in the $25 to $35 range. **Flaming
Gorge Lodge** on US 191 in Dutch John, Utah, offers
accommodations on the southeast corner of the reservoir
for those who would like to extend their stay. (801)
889-3773. There are many camping opportunities on
Flaming Gorge Reservoir. They include **Lucerne Valley**
and **Buckboard Crossing** off US 530 on the west side of
the lake. In Green River, **Tex's Travel Camp** (exit 85 off
I-80 and continue one mile east on Wyoming 374 to the
camp on Jamestown Service Road) is another possibility.
Units are $13. (307) 875-2630. There is also a state camp-
ground across from Fort Bridger (where Day 12 begins).

Food

The **Red Feather** at 211 E. Flaming Gorge Way in Green
River is a good bet for steak or chicken. (307) 875-4747.
Trudel's at 3 East Flaming Gorge Way in Green River
offers Mexican and American dishes and Friday night seafood specials. Prices are moderate and all dishes are
homemade. (307) 875-8040.

GREEN RIVER TO JACKSON HOLE

Fort Bridger, the handsomely restored Oregon Trail landmark, begins your day's Wyoming journey. Continue to
the paleontological hot spot of Fossil Butte and then
drive along the dramatic Wind River Range to Jackson
Hole, gateway to the Grand Tetons.

Suggested Schedule

8:00 a.m.	Depart Green River.
9:00 a.m.	Arrive in Fort Bridger.
10:00 a.m.	Depart Fort Bridger.
11:00 a.m.	Arrive in Fossil Butte National Monument.
12:30 p.m.	Picnic lunch in Kemmerer, home of J. C. Penney.
4:00 p.m.	Arrive Jackson Hole.

Balance of day at leisure.

Travel Route: Green River to Jackson (270 miles)
Take Interstate 80 west 52 miles to Fort Bridger. Then
return east 3 miles on Interstate 80 to Wyoming 412.
Drive north 15 miles to US 189. This road continues
north 14 miles to Kemmerer, where you take US 30 west
11 miles to Fossil Butte National Monument. Then return
to US 189, where you'll drive north along the Green
River, passing several Oregon Trail landmarks. North of
Daniel, you'll enter the Bridger-Teton National Forest and
drive along the Wind River Range, a spectacular region
for hiking and backpacking that runs along the Continental Divide. This scenic and relatively easy drive ends in
Jackson Hole.

Sightseeing Highlights
▲▲▲ **Fort Bridger**—Established as a trading post by
trapper, trader, and guide Jim Bridger in 1843, this fort
served as a supply point for emigrants on the Oregon
Trail. The fort was occupied in 1853 and 1855 by the Mormons, who retreated to Salt Lake in 1857 after skir-

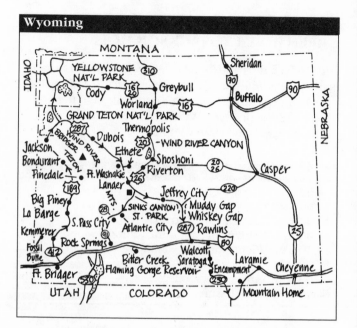

Wyoming

mishing with the federal government. American troops
took over the badly damaged site in 1857 and rebuilt the
military post using some of the original cobblestone walls
erected by the Mormons. The 29-building fort subse-
quently served as a Pony Express station, provided secu-
rity for Union Pacific work crews, functioned as a
Shoshone Indian Agency, a mining supply center, and a
garrison during the Ute Indian wars.

Now a state historic landmark, the ten restored fort
buildings mark the spot where the Oregon, Mormon, and
Pony Express trails converged. While here, you can visit
the commanding officer's quarters, the post trader's store,
the guardhouse, the post commissary, the first Wyoming
schoolhouse, and the Jim Bridger stockade. A highlight of
your visit is the commanding officer's quarters, now
restored to its original Victorian splendor. On weekends,
visitors can enjoy cookies baked in this home's wood-
fired oven. A living history program, with staff appearing
in 1880 dresses and uniforms, adds to the fun of a Fort
Bridger visit during the summer months. The fort is open

June 1 through Labor Day weekend from 8:30 a.m. to 5:30 p.m. daily and 9:00 a.m. to 4:30 p.m. on weekends the rest of the year. Grounds are open year-round. (307) 782-3842. An annual highlight is the Fort Bridger Rendezvous, a Labor Day weekend extravaganza that includes black powder shooting events, Indian wrestling, and whip fights. The fort is crowded with muzzle loaders, traders, and mountain men telling tall tales. For more information on lodging in the Fort Bridger area, see Day 11.

Fifteen miles southwest of Fort Bridger are the Piedmont charcoal kilns and ghost town, a side trip for the adventurous. Because this route requires taking several unnamed back roads, you'll want to get precise driving instructions from the rangers at Fort Bridger. As you approach the town, you'll pass three beehive-shaped kilns that produced charcoal for the Utah iron industry. In addition to the ghost town itself, you'll want to see the cemetery a quarter mile south of Piedmont.

▲▲ **Fossil Butte**—Located in the badlands 10 miles west of Kemmerer, this 8,000-acre national monument preserves one of the West's most impressive paleontological sites. Rising from multicolored red, purple, yellow, and gray Wasatch formation beds, this 1,000-foot-high butte is topped by the buff and white Green River formation, a treasure trove of fish fossils. Millions of fossils here are remnants from a series of inland lakes that once extended from the Gulf of Mexico to Alaska. The lakes dried up, leaving behind a vast treasure of 50-million-year-old fossil-bearing limestone. Paleontologists have struck it rich in this region teeming with millions of perch, herring, garpike, stingray, and catfish fossils as well as the remains of scores of other aquatic species. "Beautifully preserved fish. . .with delicate fins, tail rays, and scales all virtually undisturbed. . .are entombed here in thinly layered sediments recording the abundant life and ecology of an ancient subtropical lake," says Wilmot Bradley of the U.S. Geological Survey. Also here are insect fossils as well as remnants of an occasional turtle, bat, bird, clam, snake, or crocodile. At the visitor center you'll see portions of the abundant fossil beds that have been uncovered in limestone layers 30 to 300 feet below the butte surface. If you have extra time, take the 1.5-mile trail from the picnic area up to the top of the scenic 1,000-foot-high butte, where you can visit the fossil quarry. Back at the visitor center, scientists will demonstrate how fossils are carefully excised from limestone plates. Also here are fossil displays, videos, and ranger programs. There is handicapped access. You can picnic in an aspen grove.

Fossil Butte is open daily 8:00 a.m. to 7:00 p.m. summers and 8:00 a.m. to 4:30 p.m. the rest of the year. The beds may be inaccessible due to snowfall in the winter months. (307) 877-4455. Across the way from the monument is Ulrich's Fossil Gallery and Quarry, where you can buy a fossil or dig your own. (307) 877-6466. Another dig-your-own fossil site is Warfield Fossil Quarry south of Kemmerer west of Highway 189. The fee is $25 per day. If you intend to dig, bring sunscreen and layer your clothing against temperature changes.

▲**Fossil Country Frontier Museum**—At 400 Pine Avenue in Kemmerer, this museum has good mining exhibits as well as an intriguing collection of moonshine era stills and presses. (307) 877-6551.

▲**J. C. Penney Mother Store**—Opened in Kemmerer on April 14, 1902, by James Cash Penney and two partners, this is the birthplace of the national retail empire. The store is on Triangle Park (reached via US 189) in downtown Kemmerer, where you can also visit the Kemmerer Museum collection of fossils and artifacts from Native Americans and early settlers. You can also visit the chain store founder's home at 107 J. C. Penney Drive in the summer months or by appointment. Call the local chamber of commerce at (307) 877-3164 for details.

▲**Names Hill**—Located six miles south of La Barge on the west side of US 189, this Oregon Trail campsite was popular with pioneers, who engraved their names in the local limestone cliffs. Since this is the trail's 150th anniversary year, you won't want to miss it. Like Independence Rock on the Sweetwater and Register Cliff on the North Platte, this is a living monument to the great

westward migration, a subject we'll explore in more detail
when you visit South Pass City on Day 18.

Itinerary Option: Star Valley

A scenic alternative to our main route will provide a
memorable trip through the forested Star Valley and
Bridger-Teton National Forest and along the Snake River.
Take US 30 west from Fossil Butte to Sage. Turn north
here to Cokeville. At Border, turn onto Wyoming 89,
which leads north to US 89. Continue north through
Afton and Alpine and then follow US 26 and 89 northeast
to Hoback Junction. Pick up US 191 north to Jackson.

Highlights of this trip include the cheeseburgers and
pies at the Cheese Factory in Thayne, bird-watching in
the Cokeville area, and Periodic Spring located 7 miles
east of Afton. Take Second Avenue east from Afton and
drive 5 miles up Swift Creek Canyon to this legendary
spring.

There is free camping in the Cokeville City Park. For
more information on this route, which is 15 miles shorter
than our main route, call (307) 877-3984.

Jackson Hole

Located at the western end of your dramatic drive along
the Wind River Range, Jackson Hole will lift you out of
the wilderness and quickly put you back in the tourism
mainstream. The gateway to Grand Teton National Park,
this is one of the most popular hubs in the Rockies, a
place where discount outlets proliferate and there's a
murder a day during the summer months. This staged
event, acted out by local thespians on the Jackson town
square at 6:30 p.m., even enjoys commercial sponsorship.

This is the kind of place where you can start your day
checking out elk herds, continue with a tranquil float trip
down the Snake River, see one of the nation's best collections of Indian art, swim in a warm mountain lake, and
then top the day off with bargain hunting at a Benetton
outlet. In trying to be all things to all visitors, Jackson
Hole has become an eclectic place. Fortunately, the prox-

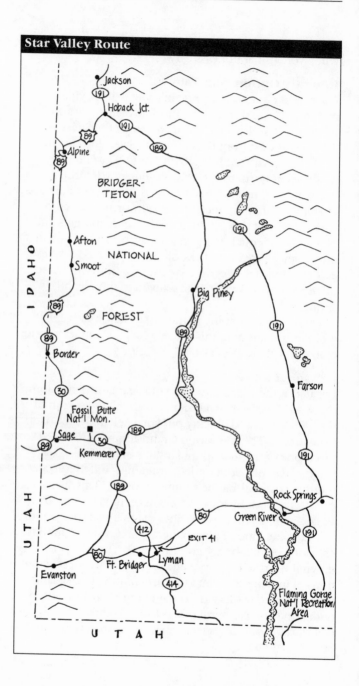

Star Valley Route

imity of this area to a major national park has confined
development to a well-contained corridor.

Named for pioneer fur trader David E. Jackson, the
name "Hole" refers to the high open valley that is surrounded by mountain peaks. In the late nineteenth century, it became an outlaw hideaway and home to cowboys and trappers. By the turn of the century, Mormon
families began to settle and civilize the town, and in 1920
it made history as the home of the first all-woman government in the nation. Gradually the area has made the
transition from fur trading and ranching center to western resort. In the process, Jackson Hole has gained many
of the amenities western travelers expect, such as dude
ranches, repertory melodramas, and candlelight dining.
But it is also a wonderful gateway to the wilderness,
home of several outstanding museums, and a great place
to relax and see wildlife.

Lodging

Due to Jackson's popularity, advance reservations are a
must in the summer months. Book as far ahead as possible.

Grand Teton National Park: Although the park
lodges are about 30 to 45 minutes north of Jackson, their
splendid setting makes them extremely popular. If your
primary interest is enjoying outdoor activities, try to
book ahead for one of these establishments. In the super-
deluxe category is **Jenny Lake Lodge**, where cabins run
$280 to 400. (307) 733-4647. **Jackson Lake Lodge**
rooms go for $79 to $135. (307) 543-2855. **Signal Mountain Lodge** charges $60 to $125 a night. (307) 543-2831,
FAX (307) 543-2569. The rustic log cabins of **Colter Bay
Village** go for $48 to $92. (307) 543-2855. Tent cabins
here rent for $19.

Jackson: The primary advantage of staying in Jackson
is its central location. It's an easy drive up to the park,
and in the evening you'll be close to restaurants, the
rodeo, shopping, and entertainment. The **Wort Hotel** at
Broadway and Glenwood downtown runs $116 to $260.
(800) 322-2727, FAX (307) 733-2067. It's within easy
walking distance of all the city's main museums and has a

comfortable lounge and restaurant. A modest and relatively quiet establishment is the **Wood's Motel** at 120 N.
Glenwood, (307) 733-2953. The **Virginian Lodge** at 750
W. Broadway, south of the downtown area, offers rooms
starting around $55. Try for one on the pool courtyard to
avoid street noise. (307) 733-2792. For a more rustic
experience, try **Twin Mountain River Ranch Bed and
Breakfast** south of town, where rooms run $55 to $75.
(307) 733-1168.

Dude Ranches: Triangle X, a working dude ranch in
Moose, offers a weekly program. (307) 733-2183. **Turpin
Meadows Ranch** north of Jackson near Moran offers
units for $100 a day or $750 per week. You'll enjoy horseback riding, fishing trips, a children's program, and cook-
outs. Facilities for the physically limited are available.
(307) 543-2496.

Camping: Campgrounds in Grand Teton National Park
open in May or June and close in September. They are
available at **Jenny Lake, Signal Mountain, Colter Bay,
Lizard Creek**, and **Gros Ventre**. All operate on a first-
come, first-served basis and charge $8 per night. **Colter
Bay** and **Flagg Ranch Trailer Villages** both offer RV
facilities. For advance reservations at Colter Bay Trailer
Village, write to Grand Teton Lodge Co., Box 240, Moran,
WY 83013. Units run $17. Call (800) 628-9988 for advance
reservations and (307) 543-2811 for reservations today.
Flagg Ranch reservations, starting at $9.50, can be made
by writing to Box 187, Moran, WY 83013, or calling (307)
543-2364. Outside Wyoming, call (800) 443-2311. Flagg
Ranch, convenient to both Grand Teton National Park
and your next destination, Yellowstone National Park,
also offers motel units and log cabins in the $60 range.
The only drawback is that it's more than an hour from
Jackson Hole.

Within the town of Jackson, **Wagon Wheel Campground** at 525 N. Cache offers units for $12.50 to $15.
(307) 733-4588. Seventeen miles south of Jackson is
Astoria Mineral Springs. Located west of Hoback Junction on US 89, this beautiful Snake River site provides
both RV and tent campgrounds. The hot springs are ideal

for those who want to kick back and will be especially popular with children. Campsites go for $14. (307) 733-2659. The Jackson Hole Area Chamber of Commerce is on North Cache Street, US 191, (307) 733-3316.

Food

For upscale dining in Grand Teton National Park, try **Jenny Lake Lodge Dining Room** on Inner Park Road. (307) 733-4647. Reservations are essential. The **Strutting Grouse** at the Jackson Hole Golf and Tennis Club, 9.5 miles northwest of Jackson, has excellent views of the Tetons. (307) 733-7788. **The Cadillac Grille** offers fish, steaks, and pasta in an art deco setting on Cache Street across from the town square. (307) 733-3279. **Bubba's** at 515 W. Broadway is popular for barbecue and breakfast. Arrive early or expect to wait. (307) 733-2288. **Tag's of Jackson** at 802 W. Broadway offers prime rib and has a special children's menu. (307) 733-7999. **Anthony's Restaurant** at 62 S. Glenwood Street specializes in northern Italian dinners. (307) 733-3717. For casual dining including pastries, soups, and sandwiches, try the **Bunnery** at 130 N. Cache. (307) 733-5474. The **Bar-T Five Covered Wagon Cookout and Wild West Show** is located one mile east of the town square on Cache Creek. Reservations are advised. (307) 733-3534.

JACKSON HOLE

This morning you'll have a chance to explore Jackson Hole and see some of its best museums. Then you'll head out to Grand Teton National Park for a wilderness hike, a chance to swim in a warm mountain lake, and a visit to one of the nation's premier Indian art collections. After watching the local shoot-out, you can choose between the Jackson Rodeo, a drama, and the Grand Teton Music Festival.

Suggested Schedule

9:00 a.m.	Jackson Hole Museum/Teton County Historical Center.
10:00 a.m.	Walking tour of Jackson.
11:00 a.m.	Wildlife of the American West Museum.
12:30 p.m.	Picnic lunch at Jenny Lake.
1:00 p.m.	Hike to String Lake and Leigh Lake.
4:00 p.m.	Colter Bay Indian Arts Museum.
6:30 p.m.	Town Square shoot-out.
Evening	Jackson Rodeo, Grand Teton Music Festival, or Jackson Hole Playhouse.

Travel Route: Jackson to Jenny Lake and Colter Bay (66 miles round-trip)

Today's itinerary begins in downtown Jackson. Head north on US 191. Five miles west of Moran Junction, pick up Teton Park Road south. Continue 8 miles to the North Jenny Lake junction and take the cutoff for Jenny Lake Lodge. Just before reaching the lodge, turn right to the String Lake Picnic Area and park. After visiting String and Leigh lakes, return north on Teton Park Road to US 191 and continue to Colter Bay. Then return south on US 191 to Jackson Hole.

Jackson Hole Sightseeing Highlights
▲▲▲**Jackson Hole Museum**—Easily spotted thanks to the Conestoga wagon on the roof, this building offers

10,000 years of regional history, from archaeological artifacts to cowboy saddles. The collection is particularly strong on the fur trade era, pioneer settlement, and trophy heads of regional animals. There's also a good display of Indian war bonnets and moccasins, fur trappers' weapons, paintings, and photographs of the town's pioneer days. The museum, located at 105 N. Glenwood Avenue behind the Wort Hotel, is open late May through September 30. Hours are Monday to Saturday 9:00 a.m. to 5:00 p.m. and Sunday 10:00 a.m. to 4:00 p.m. Admission is $2 for adults, $1 for seniors and students 6 to 18. Before leaving the museum, pick up a copy of Rachel Sidle's self-guiding tour booklet, *Historic Jackson*. It's published by the museum and costs $2. (307) 733-2414.

▲▲**Teton County Historical Center**—After leaving the Jackson Hole Museum, turn left on Glenwood Street and walk to this sister museum on Mercil Avenue. Of special interest is an exhibit focusing on Jackson Hole's status as crossroads for the western fur trade from 1807 to 1840. Here you'll learn about the Astorians, an early group of fur traders who tried to build an empire out of pelts for the richest man in America, John Jacob Astor. In the process they pioneered major portions of what would later become the principal emigration route west, the Oregon Trail. This collection also includes an excellent display of artifacts, a fine trade bead collection, and a comprehensive local history library. Open Monday through Friday. Call (307) 733-9605 for current hours.

▲▲**Jackson Walking Tour**—Leaving the museum, head south one block to the Deloney Triplets, three pioneer cabins that illustrate early Jackson Hole residential architecture. They're at 202-230 N. Glenwood Street. At 170 N. Glenwood Street, you'll see St. John's Episcopal Church and Rest House, distinguished by its unusual stockade-type bell tower, which once doubled as an ice storehouse. Across the street are Henrie's Harness and Saddle Shop and the Crane Saloon at 145 and 125 N. Glenwood Street. Next door at 105 N. Glenwood Street is the Jackson Hole Museum. Turn left on Deloney Avenue and walk one block to Cache Street. On the corner of

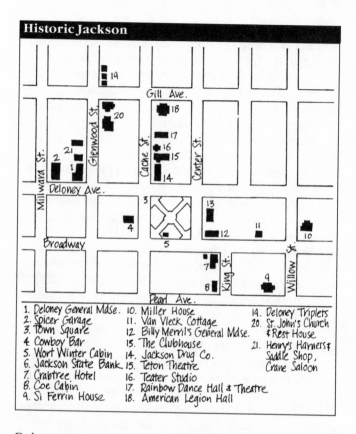

Historic Jackson

1. Deloney General Mdse.
2. Spicer Garage
3. Town Square
4. Cowboy Bar
5. Wort Winter Cabin
6. Jackson State Bank
7. Crabtree Hotel
8. Coe Cabin
9. Si Ferrin House
10. Miller House
11. Van Vleck Cottage
12. Billy Merril's General Mdse.
13. The Clubhouse
14. Jackson Drug Co.
15. Teton Theatre
16. Teater Studio
17. Rainbow Dance Hall & Theatre
18. American Legion Hall
19. Deloney Triplets
20. St. John's Church & Rest House
21. Henry's Harness & Saddle Shop, Crane Saloon

Deloney Avenue and Cache Street you may want to take a break at the old-time Jackson Drug soda fountain, where employees used to mix up soda water by rocking it back and forth in a barrel. Now in its 77th year, the fountain is known for its homemade, high butterfat ice cream. The menu also features sandwiches, chili, and bagels.

Walk north on Cache Street and you'll pass the Teton Theatre, the old log studio used by western artist Archie Teater, and Rainbow Dance Hall, now Dirty Jack's. Return north to the Town Square to visit the Wort Winter Cabin, built by the family that used to own the town's biggest hotel. Across the street at 78 E. Broadway is the Jackson State Bank, where you can inspect the old vault. Next door at 86 E. Broadway you'll see the Crabtree Hotel

building. Turn right at the corner to 85 S. King Street and
the Coe Cabin, a pioneer log building with shingled
eaves. Returning to Broadway Street, jog left to 12 Center
Street and Billy Mercill's General Merchandise building,
now home to several galleries, outfitters, and other shops.
Next door at 50-90 Center Street is The Clubhouse, an
old Jackson Hole social hub that was the scene of all-
night dances. Call the Jackson Hole Museum at (307)
733-9605 to book a guided walking tour.

▲ **Wildlife of the American West Museum**—This fine
art museum, located across the street from The Clubhouse at Deloney Avenue and Center Street, showcases
watercolors, oil paintings, and sculpture by famed artists
like Conrad Schweiring, Charles Russell, Carl Rungius,
George Catlin, and Ernest Thompson Seton. You can also
pick up information here on the Jackson Hole gallery
scene. More than two dozen art galleries are located in
and around Jackson Hole. Many are clustered within a
block or two of the Town Square. From Memorial Day to
Labor Day the museum is open Monday through Saturday
10:00 a.m. to 6:00 p.m. and Sunday 1:00 p.m. to 6:00 p.m.
The rest of the year, hours are Tuesday to Saturday 10:00
a.m. to 5:00 p.m. and Sunday 1:00 p.m. to 5:00 p.m. The
museum is closed in April and November. If you are visiting in the fall or spring, call first to make sure the museum
isn't closed. Admission is $2 for adults, $1.50 for seniors,
and $1 for students. Families pay $5. (307) 733-5771.

Grand Teton National Park

The 40-mile-long, 8- to 12-mile-wide region that is
now Grand Teton National Park has served as a hunting
ground and mountain crossroads for at least 11,000 years.
Before the arrival of the first white explorers and the
mountain men in the early nineteenth century, Indian
tribes such as the Shoshone, Gros Ventre, Flathead, and
Blackfeet all hunted in this area, described as a hole
because of the mountains that ring the high plateau. The
region was first settled by ranchers. By the end of the
nineteenth century, Jackson Hole had also become
famous for its hunting and fishing. By the 1920s, dude

ranching and tourism began to emerge as a significant business. In 1929, Congress established the 96,000-acre park embracing the main portion of the Tetons and the glacial lakes at the foot of the mountains. But local interests defeated a plan to include the Jackson Hole valley region adjacent to these promontories. Philanthropist John D. Rockefeller responded by buying up private lands in Jackson Hole for park use. Then, in 1943, President Roosevelt established the 210,000-acre Jackson Hole National Monument, which was merged with the national park in 1950. The Rockefellers complemented this expansion by donating their 33,000 acres to the park.

Rising more than a mile above the valley floor, the steep peaks are the region's principal landmarks. Laced by glacier-fed streams and pocketed by natural and man-made lakes, Jackson Hole offers easy access to the canyons, glacial valleys, waterfalls, meadows carpeted with wildflowers, and forests of pine, spruce, and fir. Deer, elk, otter, moose, beaver, and bird life all abound in this mountain wilderness. Trails ranging from short walks to challenging mountain hikes offer dramatic views of the famed Teton Peaks, formed from some of the oldest rocks in North America. For general park information, call (307) 733-2880.

Grand Teton Sightseeing Highlights

▲▲▲ **String Lake/Leigh Lake**—After lunching at the String Lake Picnic Area, hike along the east shore. The waters here are often warm enough for swimming in the summer months. Then hike about 1 mile to larger Leigh Lake. This trail continues along the east shore of Leigh Lake for another 2.8 miles to Bearpaw Lake. Enjoy as much of this path as you care to, keeping in mind that you'll be doubling back to your starting point. You'll enjoy excellent views of Mt. Moran on this route. Alternatively, you can turn left at the north end of String Lake and make the 2.4-mile-long loop back to the picnic area. Check with the rangers for route information or pick up a copy of *Short Hikes and Easy Walks in Grand Teton*

National Park by Bill Hayden and Jerry Freilich for $1 at
any of the park gift shops. After returning to your car,
drive back to Teton Park Road and rejoin US 191 to Colter
Bay.

▲▲▲ **Colter Bay Indian Arts Museum**—The shields,
moccasins, jewelry, hides, cradleboards, and hundreds of
other Native American artifacts exhibited here are among
the National Park Service's crown jewels. Highlights of
the collection include colorful pouches made from raw-
hide, a Potawatomi woman's blouse from Kansas, and an
impressive collection of Dakota Sioux instruments such
as the flutes used by men to court ladies. The collection is
the subject of a marvelous book, *The Spirit of Native
America*, by Anna Lee Walters (San Francisco: Chronicle
Books, 1989). There may be a better collection of Native
American artifacts than the one seen here. When you find
it, please drop me a line. Open 8:00 a.m. to 7:00 p.m.
daily in the summer. From late May to early June and during the month of September, hours are 8:00 a.m. to 5:00
p.m. The rest of the year hours are 8:00 a.m. to 4:30 p.m.
(307) 543-2467.

Evening Options

Begin your night on the town at the town square, where a
killing is staged promptly each evening at 6:30 p.m. Local
actors put on a good performance, but you'll need to
arrive early to get a good view of this cold-blooded shooting that comes complete with an undertaker. (307)
733-3316.

For the main event, my first choice is the Jackson Hole
Rodeo held on Wednesday and Saturday nights. Staged at
the rodeo grounds on Snow King Avenue, it features calf
roping, barrel racing, steer wrestling, and bareback and
bull riding, all scored on the official "Road" Apple computer. The bucking broncos, who earn their year's keep
for a total of perhaps three minutes of rough riding during the season (the cowboy must complete an 8-second
ride), are nature's answer to the steam catapult. A good
source of revenue for local ambulance companies, the
rodeo attracts both professionals and amateurs. It is also

the place to find out why the population of Jackson never seems to rise above the 5,000 mark. "Every time some-one has a baby," explains the droll announcer, "someone leaves town."

Rodeo admission is $8 for adults, $4.50 for children, and $21 for families. Children ages 4 to 12 are eligible to join the calf scramble. The Saturday rodeos run from late May through Labor Day. Wednesday rodeos are held from late June though Labor Day. (307) 733-2805. The rodeo starts at 8:00 p.m. and usually runs to about 10:00 p.m.

Another evening possibility in Jackson Hole is the Grand Teton Music Festival, running from mid-July to late August. (800) 786-4863. The Jackson Hole Playhouse at 145 W. Deloney Avenue offers western musicals Monday through Saturday from late May to Labor Day at 8:00 p.m. (307) 733-6994.

Helpful Hint

Teton Science School offers adult seminars and two- to six-week classes for students on natural history, botany, ecology, geology, and photography. Write to Teton Science School, Box 68P, Kelly, WY 83011, or call (307) 733-4765.

GRAND TETON NATIONAL PARK

A float trip down the Snake River, one of the best ways to see and enjoy the Teton range, begins your day. After a leisurely ride past the Tetons, you'll hike into a wilderness highlighted by waterfalls, glacial moraines, and mountain lakes. This is a day to enjoy the wildflowers and wildlife, fish for trout, and photograph some of the park's scenic highlights.

Suggested Schedule

9:00 a.m.   Snake River float trip.
12:00 noon Hike in Grand Teton National Park.
Balance of day at leisure.

Sightseeing Highlights
▲▲▲ **Snake River Float Trip**—Rafting and canoe excursions lasting from two hours to a week are offered by a dozen companies in the Jackson Hole region. You can obtain information on all the possibilities at the Jackson Hole Area Chamber of Commerce on North Cache, (307) 733-3316. Many of these companies can arrange pickup at your motel. A typical three-hour trip runs around $20, while half-day trips cost $25 to $30. Day-long trips run $40 to $50. Float trips are limited to relatively calm sections of the rivers in the park, while whitewater rides give passengers a chance to shoot the Snake rapids south of Jackson. Here are a few of the companies that can help you enjoy this famed river.

Dave Hansen Whitewater offers both full- and half-day float or whitewater trips. (307) 733-6295. Grand Teton Lodge Company at Colter Bay Village and Jackson Lake Lodge run 10-mile scenic trips with both morning and afternoon departures. A 20-mile scenic trip includes a picnic lunch. Fishing trips are also offered. (307) 543-2811. National Park Float Trips offers 10-mile scenic wildlife trips. (307) 733-6445. O.R.S. runs pleasant 1- to 7-night raft and canoe trips that include swimming, fish-

Grand Teton National Park

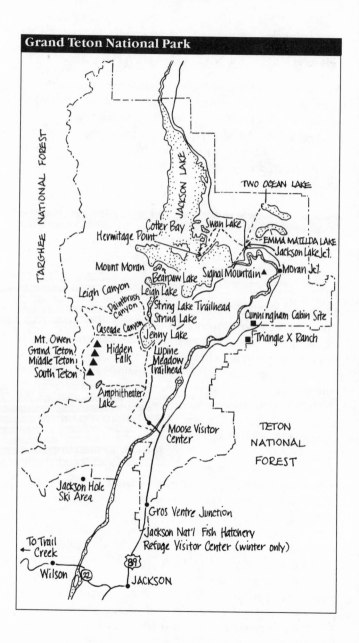

ing, hiking, camping, and combination raft/horseback or raft/wagon train trips. (307) 733-3379 or (800) 346-6277. Triangle X Float Trips operates 5- and 10-mile scenic tours throughout the day as well as lunch trips, overnight floats, and fishing trips. Special sunrise and evening wildlife watching excursions are also available. (307) 733-5500.

▲▲▲ **Hidden Falls Trail**—To enjoy this easy hike, take US 191 north to Moose and continue north on Teton Park Road to the South Jenny Lake area. Catch the shuttle boat to the west shore boat dock. (Be sure to confirm the time of the last shuttle back in the afternoon or you'll have to make the 2.5-mile return trip on foot at the end of this hike.) From here you can take the popular and (fairly steep) half-mile trail to Hidden Falls, a beautiful spot where you'll enjoy the Teton scenery, wildlife, and birdwatching. Continue uphill another 0.4 mile to Inspiration Point, where you'll have a panoramic view of the Jackson Hole region. If you get an early start on this route, you'll have time to continue another 3.5 miles on the level trail to one of the park's great scenic treasures, Cascade Canyon. The round-trip distance from the boat dock to the canyon is about 9 miles. The shuttle operates 8:00 a.m. to 6:00 p.m. in the summer for $3.50.

Itinerary Option

Here are other hikes worth special consideration during your visit to the Grand Tetons.

Hermitage Point Trails: From the Colter Bay Visitor Center on the shores of Jackson Lake, you can make the 3-mile loop walk to Hermitage Point's Swan and Heron ponds, a great place to see moose, otter, elk, beaver, sandhill cranes, trumpeter swans, and ducks. This level walk can easily be extended up to 6.5 miles by following the trail out to the end of Hermitage Point. The Colter Bay Visitor Center will offer additional information on this route. Follow the trails carefully, as unmarked paths can be confusing.

Amphitheater Lake Trail: This strenuous 9.6-mile round-trip with a 3,000-foot elevation gain begins at the

Lupine Meadow parking area off Teton Park Road south of Jenny Lake. From the meadow, you'll move up the glacial moraine through conifer forests to the edge of the tree line. The lake, located at the base of Disappointment Peak, is one of the park's scenic treasures. Be sure to consult the ranger station for weather and trail information before setting out on this six- to eight-hour trip. Rain gear and a canteen are essential.

Paintbrush Canyon Trail: This 16-mile route beginning at the String Lake Picnic Area (see Day 13 for directions) is an all-day affair for experienced hikers only. A strenuous series of glacial stair steps rises 5,000 feet up to Paintbrush Divide. As the trail's name suggests, this is a great route for wildflowers, particularly Indian paintbrush and columbine. Beautiful lakes, alpine plateaus, and streams are among the scenic highlights. Check first with the ranger station for weather and route information. Do not attempt to go beyond Paintbrush Divide, which is frequently blocked by a snow cornice. For a shorter round-trip of 12.4 miles, take this same trail to Holly Lake.

JACKSON HOLE TO YELLOWSTONE

Today a short drive north takes you to America's oldest national park, a place that looks like it was master planned by Dante and, in some locales, smells like a jackknifed truck full of rotten eggs. You'll make your way through steaming thermal fields via boardwalks and marked trails as huge explosions shoot gas, steam, and boiling water more than 100 feet into the air. Here, in the land of fire and ice, you're likely to get sprinkled by unpredictable geysers as you make your way through the geothermal citadel.

Suggested Schedule

8:00 a.m.	Depart Jackson Hole.
10:00 a.m.	Arrive Yellowstone National Park and check in.
11:00 a.m.	Old Faithful Inn.
12:00 noon	Picnic lunch.
12:30 p.m.	Upper Geyser Basin.
3:30 p.m.	Fountain Paint Pots.
6:00 p.m.	Dinner at Old Faithful Inn.
Evening	At leisure.

Travel Route: Jackson Hole to Yellowstone (96 miles)

Take US 191 north to West Thumb in Yellowstone National Park and turn left 17 miles to Old Faithful. After exploring Old Faithful and Upper Geyser Basin, drive north to Fountain Paint Pots. Remember the speed limit in the national parks is 45 mph. Be prepared for sudden stops caused by wildlife that stray onto the road.

Yellowstone National Park

While you're standing in line to buy postcards at the gift shop, a television monitor touts a $19.95 video of the park's huge 1988 fire. As you sit down for a drink at the famous Old Faithful Inn, there's a huge explosion that sends a cloud up over the hotel. Slip off a hiking trail into one of the bubbling pools and you're likely to be scalded to death. And signs all warn that "many visitors were gored last summer" by those cute buffalo that are such inviting photo subjects. Welcome to Yellowstone.

After a series of fires that burned about 793,880 acres in 1988, it's back to business as usual in America's leading thermal park. Old Faithful and more than 10,000 other thermal features continue to pack them in. Although this region has been inhabited off and on for the past 8,500 years, it was never the center of a flourishing Native American civilization. By the time the first white man, trapper John Colter, arrived in 1807, only the Sheepeaters, a mixture of Shoshone and Bannock, were located here. As park historian Aubrey Haines explains, "They lacked the horses and guns necessary to compete with their neighbors and had retreated into the mountains to live furtive, impoverished lives, even by Indian standards."

While trappers found a few pelts in this region, the fur supply soon dwindled, and by 1840 the Yellowstone Plateau was all but forgotten. Then in 1863 a gold strike in nearby Montana brought explorers back to this territory, renewing interest in the unusual geyser zones. Although there were no promising minerals here, the area was rich in thermal resources. Fascinating written accounts, paintings by landscapist Thomas Moran, and photographs by William Henry Jackson brought news of the mud volcanoes, "paint pots," fumaroles, and colorful hot springs to the nation's capital. In 1872, Congress voted to set aside 2.2 million acres of parkland in northwestern Wyoming and adjacent Montana and Idaho. Almost overnight this seemingly inhospitable wilderness flourished as a tourist attraction, a midway of geologic wonders and curiosities created over the course of 70 million years.

While similar thermal features are found in Iceland, New Zealand, and Siberia, more geysers are located in Yellowstone than in the rest of the world put together.

Lodging

Yellowstone accommodations are located in six park areas. The park's best-known and and most centrally located hotel is the **Old Faithful Inn**, offering rooms for $35 to $170. This hotel and the adjacent cabins at **Old Faithful Lodge** should be your first choice. The cabins run $19 to $31. Modern motel-style units running $56 to $60 are located at **Grant Village** on the shore of Lake Yellowstone, 17 miles east of Old Faithful. This establishment is also relatively convenient for our trip plan, although it lacks the charm of the older park hotels. On the north side of this same lake is **Lake Yellowstone Hotel**, where rooms run $66 to $260 and cabins go for $46. This is a beautiful place to stay, ideal for fishing, but it's also about an hour from the heart of the park. **Lake Lodge** cabins are $39 to $72. Several other establishments would be convenient for a longer stay but are a bit out of the way for our itinerary. Among them is **Canyon Lodge** near the Grand Canyon of the Yellowstone, where cabins run $43 to $72. On the park's north side are **Roosevelt Lodge** cabins running $24 to $49 and **Mammoth Hot Springs Hotel** where rooms run $35 to $150. Mammoth also offers cabins for $24 to $49. These hotels and cabins open between May and early June and close between Labor Day and the middle of October. **Old Faithful Snowlodge** offers winter accommodations from $35 to $47. It's important to make reservations for all these facilities as far in advance as possible. Phone (307) 344-7311 or write to Reservation Department, TW Recreational Services, Yellowstone National Park, WY 82190-9989. Don't be too picky. If you can't get your first choice, take what's available and give thanks that you got a reservation. For a list of private motels near the park, call the West Yellowstone, Montana, Chamber of Commerce at (406) 646-7701, or the Gardiner, Montana, Chamber of Commerce at (406) 848-7681.

  Camping: Eleven campgrounds operate in Yellowstone. One at Mammoth is open year-round. The rest open in May or June and close in September or October. Fees run from $6 to $10 a night. All campsites are available on a first-come, first-served basis except for Bridge Bay, which is on the nationwide Mistix Reservations system early June through Labor Day. Phone (800) 365-2267. A trailer/RV village is operated at Fishing Bridge for $18 per day. For information, call (307) 344-7311 or write TW Recreational Service, Yellowstone National Park, WY 82190. The Wyoming Travel Commission, I-25 at College Drive, Cheyenne, WY 82002, publishes a list of camping facilities in adjacent national forests. (800) 225-5996. Similar information is available from Travel Montana, Department of Commerce, Helena, MT 59620, (800) 541-1447.

Food

The **Old Faithful Inn, Lake Yellowstone Hotel, Canyon Lodge, Roosevelt Lodge**, and **Mammoth Hot Springs Hotel** all operate dining rooms. Each requires dinner reservations. There's also a restaurant and steak house at **Grant Village**. Cafeterias and snack bars operate at all major lodging areas in the park. Plan on arriving early to avoid waiting in line.

Sightseeing Highlights

▲▲▲ **Old Faithful Inn**—Distinguished by a unique atrium lobby featuring a giant fireplace, this log hotel is one of the park's authentic landmarks. Step inside and you may find a cowboy serenading a crowd from the balcony. One of the biggest log structures in the world, this hotel is also a great place to watch Old Faithful erupt and then to begin a hike out into the Upper Geyser Basin.

▲▲▲ **Old Faithful**—Although Old Faithful shows signs of losing steam—the average interval between eruptions has increased from 65 minutes to more than 75 minutes over the past 120 years—this remains the most popular show in the park. The best-known geyser in the world has two- to five-minute eruptions that can soar as high as 180 feet.

▲▲▲ **Upper Geyser Basin**—After picking up a map and checking the geyser eruption predictions at the Old Faithful Visitor Center (which also has a map of handicapped accessible facilities and features), head out to visit the world's largest geyser concentration. The Upper Geyser Basin district is easily explored by a four-mile loop walk. The self-guiding trip takes you past geysers ranging from Grotto, which erupts for 2 to 12 hours, to Giant, which has erupted 5 times since 1955. While the eruptions are the primary attraction here, it's also fun to look at some of the hot springs, such as rainbow-hued Beauty Pool and the deep blue waters of Doublet Pool. An observation point located just half a mile above Old Faithful provides an excellent overview of this steamy thermal zone. To avoid the possibility of being hurt by boiling water, you must stay on the constructed walkways as you explore this basin.

▲▲ **Fountain Paint Pots/Lower Geyser Basin Nature Trail**—This boardwalk trail is named for the bubbling mud pools and cones. Deposits of sulfur, iron oxides, arsenic sulfide, and other substances also add color to the thermal waters. In addition to the paint pots, this trail takes you to some of the park's liveliest geysers, hot pools, and fumaroles. Among them is Clepsydra Geyser, which has been erupting frequently since a 1959 earthquake.

Evening Activities

All the major park visitor centers such as Old Faithful, Mammoth, Canyon, and Grant Village operate extensive lecture programs and guided walks. Campfire talks, slide programs, one-man shows, and nature films will add to your understanding of geothermal activity, local wildlife, and the 1988 fire.

Helpful Hint

To learn more about the park's wildlife, ecology, Native American history, and geysers, sign up for a course at Yellowstone Institute, P.O. Box 117, Yellowstone National Park, WY 82190. (307) 344-7381, ext. 2384.

YELLOWSTONE NATIONAL PARK

The big burn of 1988 is the featured subject at Grant Village Visitor Center, today's first stop. Then you'll continue to Lake Yellowstone, a prime spot to view park wildlife. After a stop at the Fishing Bridge museum, you'll see more of the park's geothermal highlights, including Mud Volcano and Black Dragon's Caldron. Next, enjoy the panoramic views at Inspiration Point and Artist Point. Then hike down into the Grand Canyon of the Yellowstone.

Suggested Schedule

9:00 a.m.	1988 Fire Exhibition/Grant Village Visitor Center.
10:00 a.m.	Lake Yellowstone.
12:00 noon	Picnic lunch at Fishing Bridge.
1:00 p.m.	Mud Volcano/Black Dragon's Caldron.
2:30 p.m.	Inspiration Point.
3:00 p.m.	Artist Point/hike Grand Canyon of the Yellowstone.

Balance of day at leisure.

Travel Route

From your hotel or campground, take the Grand Loop Road to Grant Village and then continue 21 miles north to Fishing Bridge. Nine miles north are Mud Volcano and Black Dragon's Caldron. Another 7 miles north is the eastbound cutoff to Inspiration Point. Return south and exit east to South Rim Drive and Artist Point. Then drive back on South Rim Drive to the Uncle Tom's Parking Area and visit the Grand Canyon of the Yellowstone. After completing your tour, return to the same hotel where you spent the first night. Driving distance depends on where you are staying. From the Old Faithful area, the round-trip is 108 miles.

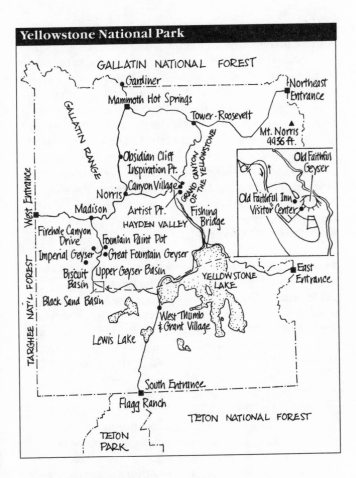

Yellowstone National Park

Sightseeing Highlights

▲▲▲**1988 Fire Exhibition/Grant Village**—Although 249 fires in 1988 burned or singed more than a third of Yellowstone's 2.2 million acres, all the park's famous attractions, including the geothermal areas and popular lodges, were spared. In addition, practically all the large mammals in Yellowstone survived the blazes. As you make your way over to Yellowstone Lake, you'll see a mosaic of brown and black cutting a deep swath across Yellowstone's verdant lodgepole pine forest. The display explains how a drought led up to this blaze fought by more than 25,000 fire fighters. The story of this dramatic battle, explained through films, brochures, self-guided boardwalk nature trails, and ranger/naturalist programs, is one of the high points of a visit to Yellowstone. Of special interest is the history of recent fire suppression, which helped build up the fuel that nurtured these blazes. As you tour, you will learn about the meadow and sage fires, the surface fires, and the devastating canopy fires that burned more than 793,880 acres. The exhibit explores some of the beneficial effects of the blaze. Already, grasses and wildflowers have begun growing in most of the burn areas, and natural reforestation efforts are also getting under way.

▲▲ **Yellowstone Lake/Fishing Bridge**—America's largest mountain lake, with over 110 miles of shoreline, this is one of the park's major wildlife hubs. It's also a fine place to enjoy Yellowstone's architectural heritage and fish for trout. Begin your visit at the Lake Yellowstone Hotel, built in 1891 and recently restored. Just south of the hotel and the Lake Village area is Bridge Bay, where you can rent fishing boats, book a guided fishing trip, or take a scenic excursion on the lake. At the Fishing Bridge Visitor Center just north of Lake Village, you'll enjoy exhibits on Yellowstone's birds, wildlife, and lake geology. (307) 344-7381, ext. 6150. While the bridge itself was closed to fishing in 1973, it's a great spot to watch summer trout spawning. Here white pelicans feed on cutthroat trout. An excellent way to explore this lake region is to drive 3 miles east of Lake Junction toward the park's east entrance. Here you'll find the Storm Point Trail on the road's south side. The 2-mile route takes you around the west side of Indian Pond, providing views of Yellowstone Lake as well as moose, marmots, and ducks. To lengthen this route, take the mile-long side trip to Pelican Creek. Rangers at the Fishing Bridge Visitor Center can provide details.

▲▲ **Mud Volcano/Black Dragon's Caldron**—This is one of the ugliest spots in the national park system. The Mud Volcano trail leads past dark, steaming Black Dragon's Caldron, which looks as if it's been stirred up by witches. The hydrogen sulfide-scented region is periodically rocked by shallow earthquakes, including a swarm that rerouted heat and steam close to the surface in 1978-79. As a result it was possible to bake dinner on the barren ground of 200-degree "Cooking Hillside." Other highlights of this trail include Sour Lake (named for its acidic water), Grizzly Fumarole, and the vile, repulsive Mud Volcano, which emitted noises that sounded like artillery fire when first discovered. Nearby is the belching Dragon's Mouth spring. Collectively, these geologic oddities add up to an offbeat thermal zone you won't want to miss.

▲▲▲ **Grand Canyon of the Yellowstone**—The brightest colors in this park are found at the Grand Canyon of the Yellowstone River. Leave your vehicle at the northernmost lot on the North Rim Drive and take the short walk to Inspiration Point. Then head over to South Rim Drive. The short Artist's Point Trail offers a wonderful view of the falls and the river descending below. Strenuous Uncle Tom's Trail descends 500 feet to the canyon floor near the lower falls. This scenic walk over stairways and paved inclines is only for hikers in good physical condition. Keep in mind that the altitude here is 8,000 feet, and keep a sharp eye out for damp or icy surfaces, which may be slippery.

YELLOWSTONE: FALLS, SPRINGS, AND GEYSERS

Three of the park's landmarks, Tower Fall, Mammoth Hot Springs, and Norris Geyser Basin, are the heart of your last day in Yellowstone. You'll also hike to the top of Mount Washburn and enjoy excellent views of wildlife and wildflowers.

Suggested Schedule

8:00 a.m.	Hike Mount Washburn Trail.
12:30 p.m.	Picnic at Tower Fall.
2:30 p.m.	Mammoth Hot Springs.
5:00 p.m.	Norris Geyser Basin.

Overnight in Yellowstone.

Travel Route

From your inn or campground, take the Grand Loop Road 5 miles north of Canyon to Dunraven Pass and the Mount Washburn trailhead. Then continue to Tower Fall and Mammoth Hot Springs. Complete your day by returning south on the Grand Loop Road to Norris Geyser Basin and Norris Museum. Return to your campsite. Again, this is a day of relatively easy driving, with heavier traffic in the vicinity of some of the popular attractions.

Sightseeing Highlights

▲▲**Mount Washburn Trail**—This 5.5-mile hike gradually ascends 1,380 feet to one of Yellowstone's best view points, the top of Mount Washburn. If you are in good physical condition, you'll find this walk a delightful way to see such wildflowers as Indian paintbrush, lupine, and phlox. Bighorn sheep are frequently grazing near the mountaintop. On top you'll enjoy a superb view of Yellowstone's lakes, canyons, peaks, and valleys. Of course, you'll also be able to see the impact of the 1988 fire.

▲▲ **Tower Fall**—Here Tower Creek descends over a breccia cliff 132 feet to the Yellowstone River. Named for handsome volcanic pinnacles, the fall attracts big crowds at the overlook. You can enjoy more privacy by trekking half a mile down to the bottom of the fall. If you have extra time, take the trail that begins half a mile north at the Calcite Springs Overlook. On this walk you'll get a good view of the springs and unusual geological formations.

▲▲▲ **Mammoth Terraces and Hot Springs**—This is my favorite spot in Yellowstone. A loop trail makes it easy to explore these fascinating formations first noted in 1839. The terraces are layers of white travertine gradually tinted orange, yellow, green, and brown by algae and bacteria growing in the hot springs runoff. Constantly changing, the Mammoth Terraces are among the most colorful spots in the park. Major features of the lower terraces include Opal Spring, Liberty Cap, Minerva Spring, and Jupiter Spring. Take an auto tour of the upper terrace (no vehicles in excess of 25 feet in length) to see White Elephant Back Terrace. Special exhibits on this region can be seen at Mammoth's Albright Visitor Center. Call (307) 344-7381, ext. 2357, for details.

Itinerary Option

The 45th Parallel Hot Springs, commonly called Boiling River, is a beautiful spot to relax. Open year-round, except for roughly six weeks in the spring, the water rushes down into the Yellowstone River. Look for a safe pool or eddy in the rocks where you can enjoy the 100-degree thermal water. To reach the 45th Parallel, drive north from Mammoth 3 miles toward Gardiner, Montana. You'll see a sign for the parking lot. Follow the trail south. The 45th Parallel is easy to spot thanks to the steam rising off the river. There's no admission charge. (307) 344-7381.

Norris Geyser Basin—The hottest, most volatile geyser basin in North America, Norris features the world's tallest geyser, Steamboat. Completely unpredictable, this

geyser can erupt as high as 300 to 400 feet, showering
hundreds of innocent bystanders in the process. Another
big winner here is Echinus Geyser, which erupts every 30
to 80 minutes. This rare acid water geyser has a pH level
that's almost as low as vinegar. Cistern Spring, a lovely
blue pool, and Emerald Spring are two of Norris's scenic
highlights. Don't miss Porcelain Terrace, where you can
see a large number of colorful and noisy vents. With luck,
you could even see a geyser being born here. The Norris
Museum, open 8:00 a.m. to 6:00 p.m. from June 11 to
August 26, offers informative exhibits on this geyser basin.
Call (307) 344-7733.

Just west of Yellowstone National Park is Gallatin National Forest, your gateway to a 10-day extension of the primary itinerary. This loop trip, which can be added to the basic 22-day trip or substituted for days that do not fit into your schedule, will show you some of the best-known destinations in the Rockies, including Glacier National Park, the Sawtooth National Recreation Area, and Sun Valley. Also along the way are lesser-known highlights such as the Missoula Smoke Jumpers Center, the National Bison Range, the estimable restaurant at Whitefish Lake golf course, Bob Scriver's sculpture gallery in Browning, the Idaho ghost town of Bonanza, and Craters of the Moon National Monument. Every one of these destinations is well worth your time and will add to your enjoyment of the Rocky Mountain region. By following my plan, you can rejoin the main itinerary on Day 18. Of course, if you only want to take part of this extension to, say, Glacier National Park, simply double back to the primary itinerary whenever you'd like.

First Day: Yellowstone to Anaconda (196 miles)
Head west from Madison Junction 14 miles to West Yellowstone. Take US 287 north and west 85 miles to the old nineteenth-century territorial capital of **Virginia City** and the neighboring town of **Nevada City**. These restored mining camps offer a good look at the state's pioneer, mining, and ranching past. After touring Virginia City's twenty restored buildings, including an old pharmacy, Wells Fargo office, and newspaper, visit the **J. Spencer Watkins Memorial Museum** at 219 W. Wallace Street. It's open daily 9:00 a.m. to 6:00 p.m. during the summer. Also in Virginia City is the **Opera House** at 340 W. Wallace. Plays and melodramas are staged Tuesday through Sunday in the summer months. It costs $10 for adults and $5 for children. (406) 843-5377. You can ride over to **Nevada City** during the summer months on the **Alder**

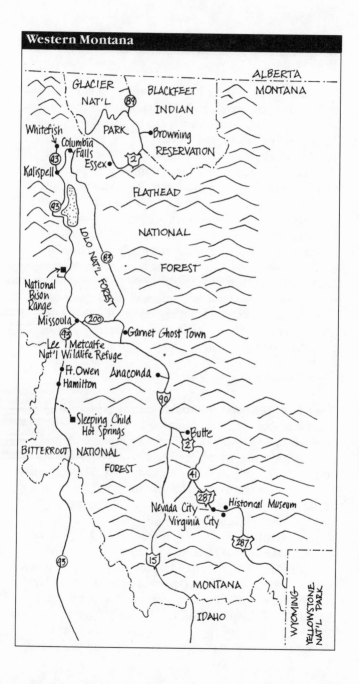

Western Montana

Gulch Short Line train. The fare is $3 for adults, $1.50 for children. Be sure to see the mechanical music machines at the town music hall.

Continue north on US 287 another 28 miles to Montana 41. Then drive north 20 miles and pick up Montana 2 west another 20 miles to **Butte**. In Butte, stop by the Chamber of Commerce at 2950 Harrison Avenue and pick up information on walking and driving tours of this town and its historic districts. (406) 494-5595. On the two-hour self-guiding uptown tour, you'll see some of the town's famous mansions and churches as well as the courthouse and first copper mine. Highlights include the **Copper King Mansion** at 219 W. Granite, a 32-room Victorian open 9:00 a.m. to 5:00 p.m. $5 for adults and $3.50 for children. (406) 782-7580. **The World Museum of Mining and Hell Roaring Gulch** on West Park Street is a 12-acre museum that includes memorabilia from the city's copper heyday and a mining camp village that re-creates the town's formative years. (406) 723-7211. Also in Butte is the **"Old Number One" train tour** to the mining museum and the edge of the Berkeley Pit. Take exit 211 off I-90 to **Fairmont Hot Springs Resort**. Check into one of the $72 to $160-a-night rooms at this resort, which offers you a choice of four hot springs pools. (406) 797-3241 or, in Montana, (800) 221-3272. Seventeen miles west on I-90 is **Anaconda**, the showplace town created by copper king Marcus Daly. You can spend the night here at the **Vagabond Lodge Motel** at 1421 East Park Street, where rooms run $32 to $50 a night. (406) 563-5251. **The Lost Creek Campground**, 1.5 miles east of Anaconda on Montana 1, has unimproved units. In Deer Lodge, **Indian Creek Campground** has complete facilities including a fishing pond. Units start at $14. Take exit 184 off I-90. (406) 846-3848.

Second Day: Anaconda to Missoula (137 miles)
Take the **Anaconda Historical Circle Tour Bus** that shows off this town's Romanesque, Victorian, and art deco highlights. (406) 563-2400. Then stop by the visitor center at 306 East Park Street to learn more about the

town's past. (406) 563-2400. Also worth a visit is the
Copper Village Museum and Arts Center at 401 East
Commercial Street. (406) 563-2422. From Anaconda,
return east 9 miles to I-90. Continue north 17 miles to
Deer Lodge. Take exit 184 to the **Grant-Kohrs Ranch
National Historic Site.** Hourly guided tours show you
the ranch house from 10:00 a.m. to 7:30 p.m. in the summer and 10:00 a.m. to 4:00 p.m. the rest of the year. You
can also take a self-guiding ranch tour. On your visit to
this working cattle ranch, you'll see remnants of this
empire, which ran cattle all the way to Canada. There are
thirty period buildings here, a big wagon collection, a
blacksmith shop, and the vast (23-room) ranch house.
(406) 846-2070. Also in Deer Lodge at 1106 Main Street is
the **Old Montana Prison** where a drama group offers
plays inside the walls. (406) 846-3111.

At Philipsburg, visit the **Ghost Town Hall of Fame
Museum**, which offers an overview of extinct Montana
towns.

Your next stop is **Garnet**, an 1870s gold camp that is
now one of Montana's finest ghost towns. To reach it,
continue west on I-90 another 46 miles to the Bearmouth
exit. Drive 6 miles east to Bear Gulch Road. Continue
north 10 miles on this unpaved road (no trailers or large
RVs, exercise caution) to the town site. Named for the
ruby-colored stones found in the area, Garnet features
more than fifty buildings in a state of arrested decay. For
visitor information, call (406) 329-3914 or 721-4269.
Small cabins are available for rent here (one is a former
speakeasy). Return to I-90 and drive 33 miles east to **Missoula**, home of the University of Montana and the **U.S.
Forest Service's Smoke Jumpers Center**. Take Broadway (Business Route 90) west 7 miles to the Missoula Airport terminal. Just beyond the terminal entrance you'll
reach the smoke jumpers base. Exhibits, films, and
interpretive displays tell the story of aerial fire fighting.
This base is home to a mix of short- and long-term work-
ers who fly all over the West putting out fires. Their job is
to get in quickly and put out little blazes before they rage
out of control. On a busy day, fire fighters will make

as many as three jumps, catching a helicopter ride back to the office at the end of each assignment. (406) 329-4934.

For a drink and a chance to enjoy the sunset, why not try the **Greenough Mansion**, where you'll enjoy one of the best views in town. Return downtown on Broadway and turn right on Reserve Street. Turn right on South Street to Fort Missoula. Then return to Reserve Street, turn right and head to 39th Street. Turn left on this street, which turns into S.W. Higgins. Continue to Pattee Creek and turn right to Whitaker Street. Turn right again and follow this street, which becomes Whittier Street, until it hits Ben Hogan Drive. Turn left to the Greenough Mansion (yes, this is the most direct route). Try for a seat on the veranda. **The Mansion** restaurant here is also a good upscale spot for dinner. (406) 728-5132.

In town, the **Pacific Grill** at North Higgins and Rail Road has a pleasant outdoor beer garden. (406) 542-3353.

A good place to spend the night on the Clark Fork River is **Goldsmith's Inn** at 809 East Front Street. Rooms run $61 to $78. (406) 721-6732. It's adjacent to **Goldsmith's Premium Ice Cream**, where cones, sundaes, breakfast, lunch, and desserts are served on a riverfront patio. **Holiday Inn Missoula Parkside** at 200 Pattee Street offers rooms for $55 to $75. (406) 721-8550.

The Birchwood Hostel at 600 South Orange Street in Missoula runs $6 a night. (406) 728-9799. **Jim and Mary's RV Park** at 9800 Highway 93 north has complete facilities starting at $14. (406) 549-4416. No tents, and no children.

Third Day: Missoula to Kalispell/Glacier National Park (162 miles)

Take I-90 west 9 miles to US 93. Continue north 28 miles to Ravalli and then head west 6 miles to the **National Bison Range**. This 19,000-acre preserve is home to descendants of America's oldest living residents. Since the first bison arrived on our continent 25,000 years ago from Asia via the Bering Strait land bridge, they have roamed a region extending from Canada's Great Slave Lake to Mexico.

This preserve offers excellent driving trails where you can see buffalo, elk, bighorn sheep, bobcats, badgers, deer, beavers, pronghorn, and many other species. The 19-mile-long **Red Sleep Mountain drive** is one of the best ways to view wildlife in the Rockies. It takes about two hours. An interpretive center tells the tragic story of the near extinction of our country's 50 million buffalo in the nineteenth century. (406) 644-2211.

Return to US 93 and drive north 31 miles to Polson. If you're eager to see wildlife, continue to **Big Arm Resort and Marina**. For about $35 you can rent a fishing boat and head across to **Wild Horse Island**, an undeveloped state park. Once used by the Flathead and Pend d'Oreilles to safeguard their horses from Blackfeet, the island now has a herd of about 100 bighorn sheep. Also here are eagle nests and wildflowers. Fishing is permitted with state and tribal licenses. Remember that sudden storms are always a possibility on Flathead Lake. Use caution when motoring across to the island, and be sure to get the weather forecast before setting out.

Continue north 40 miles on US 93 to Kalispell, home of one of the most fascinating historic homes in the state, the **Conrad Mansion**. A Norman-style home built by pioneer Missouri River trader C. E. Conrad, it's furnished with sleigh beds, canopied four-posters, and original Chippendale furniture. It's worth a visit just to marvel at the wood-paneled interior. The mansion on Woodland Avenue at 3rd Street is open May 15 to June 14 and Sept. 15 to Oct. 15, 10:00 a.m. to 5:30 p.m. From June 15 to Sept. 15, hours are 10:00 a.m. to 8:00 p.m. Closed balance of the year. (406) 755-2166.

Continue north 30 miles on US 2 to **Glacier National Park**. My favorite restaurant in this area is **Whitefish Lake Restaurant** at the Whitefish Lake Golf Club, about an hour west of Glacier National Park. Smoked pork chops with champagne mustard and applesauce, Montana lamb chops, baby back ribs, and fish and vegetable entrées are all good. It's across the street from the **Grouse Mountain Lodge**, 1205 Highway 93 West, where rooms run $90. (406) 862-3000, FAX (406) 756-1271, in Montana and (800) 321-8822 outside Montana. In Kalispell, you can spend the night at the **White Birch Motel** at 17 Shady Lane, where rooms run $30 to $55. (406) 752-4008. Also in Kalispell, **Stillwater Inn** at 206 4th Avenue East offers rooms in the $40 to $75 range. (406) 755-7080. **The North Fork Hostel** in Polebridge, just west of Glacier National Park, runs $12. (406) 756-5174. On the south side of Glacier Park is the **Izaak Walton Inn at Essex**. This former railworkers' hotel is now popular with park visitors. The restaurant is filled with rail memorabilia, and you're served by employees wearing bib overalls. At night you'll drift off to the sounds of train whistles blowing in the adjacent Burlington Northern yard. (406) 888-5700. Rooms start around $65.

In Glacier National Park, accommodations are available at six locations. On the west side of the park, the **Village Inn** at Apgar is $65 to $96. **Lake McDonald Lodge** has units running $53 to $94. On the east side, **Glacier Park Lodge** at East Glacier offers rooms from $82 to $151, as does **Many Glacier Hotel**. **The Rising Sun Motor Inn**, 7 miles west of the St. Mary's park entrance, offers rooms for $53 to $65, and the **Swiftcurrent Motor Inn**, 1 mile west of Many Glacier Hotel, has rooms for $23 to $65. More remote possibilities are the **Sperry** and **Granite Park** chalets accessible to backpackers in the summer. You can book any of the hotels by calling (406) 226-5551 from May to September. From October to May, call (602) 207-6000. Inside Montana, call (800) 332-9351. To reserve the two chalets, call (406) 888-5511. Write to the park at West Glacier, MT 59936, for more information.

Camping is available at thirteen sites in Glacier National Park. Campgrounds that can be reached by paved road are Apgar, Avalanche Creek, Fish Creek, Many Glacier, Rising Sun, St. Mary, Two Medicine, and Sprague Creek. Trailer space is available at all but Sprague Creek. Campgrounds accessible by gravel road are River, Bowman Creek, Bowman Lake, Cut Bank Creek, Kintla Lake, Logging Creek, and Quartz Creek. All campsites are on a first-come, first-served basis. There are no showers in the park campgrounds, but you can use facilities at Rising Sun and Swiftcurrent motor inns.

In East Glacier, the **Bison Creek Ranch** offers cabins for $30 a night. (406) 226-4482. Family-style dinners are available. For information on accommodations outside the park, contact the **Flathead Convention and Visitor Association**, (800) 543-3105.

Fourth Day: Glacier National Park

Glacier Park and adjacent Waterton Lakes National Park in Alberta have been designated the first International Biosphere Reserve by UNESCO. As soon as you enter the park, you'll see why. The steep mountains, deep glacial valleys, lakes, wildlife, trails, and dramatic drives such as the 50-mile-long Going to the Sun Highway create many outdoor opportunities. There are pack trips, naturalist guided hikes, boat tours, fishing, backpacking, swimming, and cycling possibilities as well as an 18-hole golf course at West Glacier near the park boundary. Most of the park is wilderness where you're likely to spot mountain goats, elk, moose, black bears, deer, and bighorn sheep. In the summer, the park's alpine region offers some of our continent's finest wildflower viewing dominated by heather, glacier lily, and bear grass.

A good place to begin your visit is the **Apgar Visitor Center**, where you can pick up trail information. Then continue 10 miles east on the **Going to the Sun Highway** to visit **Lake McDonald Lodge**. This log building, with its cedar colonnade and Indian handicrafts, is a delight. Here, lobby guests sitting beneath the watchful eyes of mounted animals are warmed by a massive stone fireplace inscribed with Indian pictographs. You can book a tour on one of the classic White Motorcoach buses from the 1930s which ferry visitors around on sightseeing trips. Convertible tops make these the ideal rubbernecking vehicles. Another possibility is the hour-long boat tour of Lake McDonald that departs from the lodge.

Continue east on the Going to the Sun Highway to the Avalanche campground. Here you can take the 1.6-mile **Trail of the Cedars** along Avalanche Creek. Return to the highway and continue to the Logan Pass Visitor Center. Here a 2.6-mile round-trip leads to the **Hidden Lake**

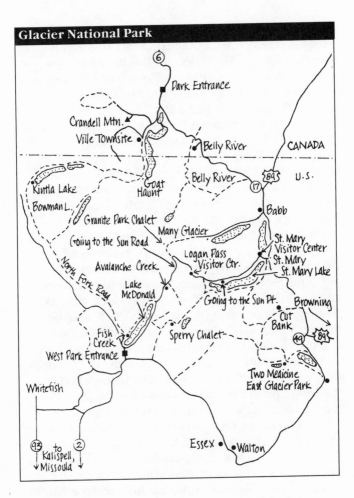

Glacier National Park

overlook. This is a good place to spot wildlife, water-falls, and, of course, Glacier's dramatic peaks. The trail makes a 500-foot elevation gain.

Fifth Day: Glacier National Park and Browning (145 miles)

Today you'll explore the east side of the park including the **St. Mary Lake area**. One of the most picturesque spots in the Rockies, it was chosen as the setting for a film based on Jack London's *White Fang*, set during the

Alaskan gold rush. When asked why he didn't just go back to Skagway, setting of the original story, the producer explained, "Alaska doesn't look like Alaska anymore." Fortunately, Montana still looks like Montana, as you'll discover on your 3-mile round-trip to St. Mary Falls and Virginia Falls. Begin at the St. Mary Falls pullout on the south side of the Going to the Sun Highway. Next, drive out of the park at St. Mary and head north on US 89 for 9 miles to **Babb**. Then drive west 12 miles to Many Glacier Hotel. This is another popular hiking area. A 2.5-mile hike circling Swiftcurrent Lake begins at the Many Glacier Hotel. Another possibility is the hike to Redrock Falls, which begins at the end of the Many Glacier Road near the parking lot for the Swiftcurrent Coffee Shop and Camp Store. This 3.6-mile round-trip is a great way to see the park's backcountry. At this point my itinerary heads out of the park to **Browning**, but if you have an extra day and would like to see the Waterton Lake area, you can return to Babb, head north 4 miles on US 89, and then pick up Montana 17 west 34 miles to **Waterton Park** in Canada. Among the highlights here is the 1.9-mile round-trip hike to **Rainbow Falls**. It leaves in the vicinity of the ranger station near the boat dock on the south end of Waterton Lake. If you choose to add Waterton to your trip, allow at least a day to explore this park.

If you don't add Waterton to your trip, return from the Many Glacier area to Babb. Take US 89 south and make the 31-mile descent to the Great Plains and Browning. Anyone who visits Glacier National Park and doesn't make the hour-long side trip to the **Bob Scriver Studio and Wildlife Museum** at the intersection of US 89 and US 2 is missing one of the state's authentic treasures. Living on the Blackfeet Reservation where he was raised, Scriver, now 77, began doing his bronze sculptures at the age of 43 after a career as a school bandleader and a taxidermist. Much of his time has been dedicated to preserving Blackfeet traditions at his Browning museum. An entire wing of his museum is devoted to sculptures and exhibits on traditions, customs, and ceremonies of this tribe. Another is devoted to his taxidermy, while a third focuses on Scriver sculptures ranging from Lewis and Clark to Buffalo Bill. Of special interest is his 52-piece "No More Buffalo" gallery, which looks at a 1,200-year span of Blackfeet history. Scriver's studio and museum has been a spawning ground for a new generation of Blackfeet artists. "Not that they need my help," he says. "The Crow, the Sioux, all the Indian tribes have produced great artists. But the Blackfeet are just intuitive, the best I've ever seen." The museum is open daily 8:00 a.m. to 5:00 p.m. May though September and by appointment at other times of the year. (406) 338-5425. Also here is the **Museum of the Plains Indians**, (406) 338-2230. There you'll see an oustanding collection of Blackfeet treasures and learn about other tribes that dominated this region. Return west 43 miles on US 2 to Essex and dine at the **Izaak Walton Inn**. Stay overnight here, at Glacier Park 29 miles away, or in the Whitefish/Kalispell Area.

Sixth Day: Glacier National Park to Hamilton/ Bitterroot Valley (220 miles)

Take US 2 south 15 miles from West Glacier and take Montana 206 south 10 miles to Montana 35. Continue 14 miles to Bigfork and take Montana 209 east 5 miles to Montana 83, the Swan Highway. Continue south 91 miles along the Swan Range, passing wildlife refuges, mountain lakes, and resort areas until you reach Montana 200. Turn east and drive 33 miles to Missoula. Incidentally, if you skipped Garnet ghost town on Day 2, there's another dirt road approach off Montana 200, 9.6 miles west of the Montana 200/Montana 83 junction. Drive 12 miles southeast on the Garnet Range Road. When you reach the Garnet sign, continue another mile on an unimproved road to the ghost town.

After returning to Montana 200, continue south on US 93 for 27 miles to the **Lee Metcalf National Wildlife Refuge**. This 2,700-acre preserve on the east bank of the Bitterroot River north of Stevensville is a gem. Take some time to hike the wooded trails past the beaver ponds and streams and you'll be rewarded with views of osprey, great blue herons, sandhill cranes, and perhaps a whistling swan or two. Deer, moose, and an occasional bear are also seen in this refuge, which offers great views of the surrounding Bitterroot Mountains.

Continue south 1 mile to Stevensville. At the corner of 4th and Charles streets is **Fort Owen**, a kind of nineteenth-century time capsule located ½ mile east of U.S. 93 at the Stevensville Junction. (406) 542-5500. Lewis and Clark were the first white men to visit this area. They were followed by missionaries who began proselytizing the Flathead Indians in 1841. In 1850, Major John Owen created his fort, the first white settlement in Montana. Later, Fort Owen became a farming and trading center. Excellent interpretive displays give a good sense of this area's evolution. A mile away at the west end of 4th Street in Stevensville is **St. Mary's Mission**, which was established in 1841. This collection focuses on the mission's work with the Flathead. Art and artifacts are displayed. Open 1:00 p.m. to 5:00 p.m. daily from April 15 to October 15. Admission is $2 for adults and $1 for children. (406) 777-5734.

Another 20 miles south on Montana 269 is **Hamilton**, the town built by Marcus Daly, the copper king who also created Anaconda. At 251 East Side Highway (Montana 269) you'll come to the 42-room **Daly Mansion**. Set on a 20,000-acre site against a Bitterroot Mountain backdrop, this Georgian Revival-style house has 24 bedrooms, 15 bathrooms, and 7 Italian marble fireplaces. It is landscaped with exotic trees from throughout the world, and it retains portions of the grand horse farm where Daly produced champion thoroughbreds that raced on his tracks in Anaconda and Butte. The museum is open daily from May 1 to September 30. Admission is $5 for adults and $2 for children. (406) 363-6004. If you have extra time, consider driving southeast of town on a dirt road (no RVs or trailers) to **Sleeping Child Resort**. This resort has an open pool, hot tubs, and a sauna. (406) 363-6250. Lodging is also available.

In Hamilton the **Best Western** at 409 First Street has rooms for $42 to $56. (406) 363-2142. In Sula, 32 miles south of Hamilton, the **Broad Axe Lodge** at 1237 East

Fork Road has lodge rooms for $55 to $65 a night. The lodge is on the east fork of the Bitterroot River, surrounded by national forest. (406) 821-3878. Also in Sula, the **Lost Trail Hot Springs Resort** on US 93 offers rooms for $45 to $55. (406) 821-3574. There's camping at **Black Bear Forest**, an improved Forest Service campground 13 miles east of US 93 on Montana 38. **Lick Creek Campground**, 11 miles south of Hamilton at 4129 US 93, has complete facilities. Units run $7 to $10. (406) 821-3840. In Hamilton, the **Coffee Cup Cafe** at 500 S. First Street is a good family-style restaurant. (406) 363-3822. Also try **4B's** for family dining, at 1105 N. First Street, (406) 363-4620.

Seventh Day: Hamilton to Stanley, Idaho (228 miles)

Drive south 45 miles on US 93 through the Bitterroot National Forest to the Idaho line. Here at the Continental Divide, you'll continue south another 46 miles to **Salmon**, the state's whitewater capital and birthplace of Sacajawea. Lewis and Clark, who crossed the Continental Divide at this point, called the Salmon "The River of No Return." It flows through one of the biggest wilderness areas in the continental United States. In the town of Salmon you can book a whitewater trip running from a day to a week. A ride through steep river gorges is a great way to spot elk, deer, and other wildlife. The fishing is terrific. Drop by the **Salmon Chamber of Commerce** at 200 Main Street for a complete list of rafting companies and outfitters. (208) 756-4935.

Continue south and west via US 93 and Idaho 74 for 115 miles through the Salmon and Challis national forests. The last 55 miles into Stanley are fairly slow going due to the serpentine roadway, but this gives you more time to enjoy the great views. Fishermen will be frequently tempted to pull off and try their luck in the Salmon waters. At Sunbeam, 42 miles west of Challis on Idaho 75, pick up the dirt road (no large RVs or trailers) for the 9-mile drive up to the old **Yankee Fork Gold Dredge**. For $2 you can take a tour of the last of sixty dredges that

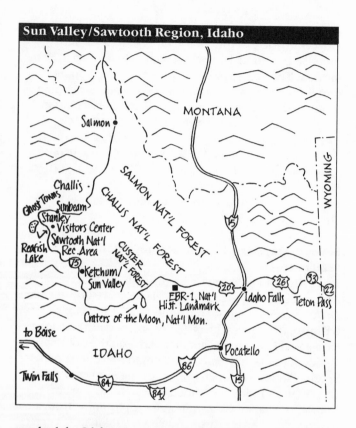

Sun Valley/Sawtooth Region, Idaho

worked the Idaho rivers over the past century. Continue beyond the ghost town of Bonanza to **Custer**, one of the most inviting historic towns in the Rockies. This handsome restoration includes the old stamp mill, blacksmith shop, jail, saloon, livery stable, rooming house, mercantile store, and cemetery. A small museum here will provide you with a self-guided tour brochure on this town, founded in 1878 in memory of General George Armstrong Custer. The museum is open from July 1 to September 5 from 10:00 a.m. to 5:00 p.m.

After completing your visit to Custer, return to Idaho 75 and drive to **Stanley**, hub of the Sawtooth National Recreation Area. A good place to dine is the **River Company Restaurant** on the Salmon River in Stanley. Another possibility is **Mountain Village Restaurant** on

Idaho 21 at Idaho 75. (208) 774-2222. The **Sawtooth Hotel and Cafe** at the west end of Main Street serves breakfast and lunch. (208) 774-9947. This bed and breakfast also offers rooms for $21.50 to $60. **Mountain Village Lodge** at Idaho 21 and Idaho 75 has rooms for $42 to $110. (208) 774-3661 or (800) 843-5475. **Idaho Rocky Mountain Ranch**, 9 miles south of Stanley on Idaho 75, runs $80 to $120. (208) 774-3544. **Redfish Lake Lodge**, on Redfish Lake Road, 5 miles south of Stanley off Idaho 75, charges $42 to $200. (208) 774-3536. There are twenty-six campgrounds in the Stanley area. Among them are National Forest sites such as **Basin Creek** on the Salmon 8.9 miles east of Stanley on Idaho 75 and **Salmon River** 5.1 miles east of Stanley on the same road. Stop at the **Redfish Lake Visitors Center** just south of Stanley on Idaho 75 and you'll get information on eleven Forest Service campgrounds in this area such as **Redfish Point** and **Redfish Outlet**. Call the recreation area office at (208) 726-8291 for more details on camping and exploring this region. Additional details are available from the Stanley-Sawtooth Chamber of Commerce, which is also a good source of information on local rafting companies. (208) 774-3411. Or write to P.O. Box 8, Stanley, ID 83278.

Eighth Day: Stanley to Sun Valley (61 miles)

Charles Kuralt of "On the Road" fame was once asked to name his favorite spot in America. Without hesitation, he suggested somewhere in the Idaho mountains such as the **Sawtooth National Recreational Area**. Today you'll have a chance to explore the beauty of this 216,000-acre wilderness known for its gorges, waterfalls, meadows, and glacial basins. Many companies based in Stanley offer whitewater trips on the Salmon River. **The River Company** at (208) 774-2244 and **Triangle C Ranch** at (208) 774-2266 are two of the possibilities. One-day trips run about $70 with half-day trips starting around $45. More than 300 miles of trails offer easy access for backpackers. There's fishing on four major rivers that head into the wilderness as well as opportunities for whitewater raft-

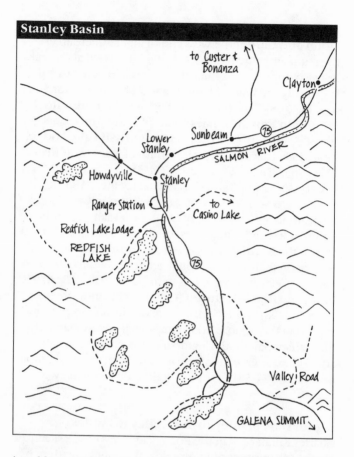

Stanley Basin

to Custer & Bonanza

Clayton

Lower Stanley

Sunbeam

75

SALMON RIVER

Howdyville

Stanley

Ranger Station

to Casino Lake

Redfish Lake Lodge

REDFISH LAKE

75

Valley Road

GALENA SUMMIT

ing. Mountain bike and pack trip possibilities also abound in this region. At the Redfish Lake Visitor Center, you can pick up information on the **Sawtooth Scenic Route** south to Sun Valley. It's open 9:00 a.m. to 6:00 p.m. daily in the summer. (208) 774-3376. A cassette recorder with a narrated tape on your route is also available here at no charge. You'll drop it off at the south end of the recreation area. Along the way are many promising side trips. For example, Redfish Lake rents boats and has good swimming beaches as well as trail rides. Near the Redfish Visitor Center, a 1.25-mile drive east of Idaho 75 takes you up Boundary Creek to the trailhead for the 4-mile round-trip hike to Casino Lakes. Another good possibility is the **Williams Creek Mountain Bike Trail** that begins about 7 miles south of the Redfish Lake Visitor Center. Near the top of Galena Summit, the 4-mile round-trip hike west to Titus Lake is a winner. Look for the parking sign on Idaho 75 denoting the trailhead. If you have more time, a four-wheel-drive road cuts off Idaho 75 and heads up Boulder Creek. This road, near the southern end of the recreation area, terminates at a trailhead, where you can hike about 5 miles round-trip to Boulder Lakes, gateway to the White Cloud Mountains.

Continue south to **Sun Valley**, the ski resort created in the Great Depression by W. Averell Harriman, chairman of the Union Pacific railroad. The birthplace of the chair lift and a favorite of celebrities from Harry Truman (he fished locally with his suit and hat on) to Jackie Kennedy, Sun Valley is adjacent to Ketchum, the town that once ranked second only to Sydney, Australia, in sheep shipping. Although the emphasis in Sun Valley is on recreation, you don't have to get physical. Sun Valley offers a summer music festival in late June and July and Saturday night ice shows starring world-class performers in the summer. There are also a number of fine galleries as well as the Ore Wagon Museum, which offers a look at the region's mining history.

Sun Valley Lodge, where Ernest Hemingway finished *For Whom the Bell Tolls*, is an essential part of any visit to this region. One morning in the fall of 1941 the author, a passionate hunter, interrupted his morning shave to respond to the sound of honking geese flying above the resort's front door. Rushing out in his pajamas, he hit a goose that landed on the lawn next to the lodge pond. No one was more startled by this shooting than Hemingway's third wife, Martha Gellhorn. "Good God, Ernest," she asked, "you didn't shoot John Boettinger (a hunting partner and Franklin D. Roosevelt's son-in-law), did you?"

Hemingway, who lived in this resort community from 1958 until he took his life in 1961, is buried in a cemetery on the north side of town. There's also a **Hemingway memorial**, a mile up from the Sun Valley Lodge on Trail Creek. At this site you'll find a small bust and an epitaph originally written by Hemingway for a young friend who died in a hunting accident: "Best of all he loved the fall . . . the leaves yellow on the cottonwoods, leaves floating on the trout streams and above the hills, the high blue windless skies. . . . Now he will be part of them forever."

It's still possible to visit some of Ernest Hemingway's old haunts like **Whiskey Jacques** on Ketchum's Main Street (in his day it was known as the Alpine), but a better place to explore the legend is the historical collection at the community library.

Sun Valley Lodge is the best place to stay in this area. Rooms start at $95 a night. (800) 786-8259. You'll have use of the resort's recreation facilities, be able to take advantage of the ice rink, and see free movies like *Sun Valley Serenade*. The **Ketchum Korral Motor Lodge** at 310 S. Main Street offers rooms from $50 to $90. (208) 726-3510. **Best Western Tyrolean Lodge** at 308 Cottonwood runs $55 to $75. (208) 726-5336. The **River Street Inn** at 100 River Street offers bed and breakfast for $100 to $150. (208) 726-3611. The **Sun Valley Chamber of Commerce**, at (208) 726-3423 or (800) 634-3347 nationwide, books rooms at many local establishments.

Camping is available at two sites in the Sawtooth National Recreation Area on Idaho 75 north of Sun Valley. They are **Park Creek**, 12 miles from town, and **Phi Kappa**, 15 miles away. Both are improved sites with water, fireplaces, and rest rooms. For a full-service campground, try the **Sun Valley RV Resort** 1 mile south of town on Idaho 75, where tent and RV sites run $15 to $17. (208) 726-3429.

Louie's Pizza at 331 Leadville in Ketchum is a good choice for Italian dining at moderate prices. Arrive early to beat the line. (208) 726-7775. The **Pioneer Saloon** at 300 N. Main Street in Ketchum is a popular steak and seafood establishment, and you need to arrive early if you don't want to wait. (208) 726-3149. For an upscale meal, try the **Lodge Dining Room** at Sun Valley Lodge. (208) 622-4111. Deck dining featuring steaks and seafood is available at the **Ore House** on Sun Valley Mall. (208) 622-4363.

Ninth Day: Sun Valley

This is a day at leisure in the Sun Valley area. Enjoy hiking, rafting, fishing, riding, or swimming, or just relax. Try fly-fishing along Silver Creek, Big Wood River, or Trail Creek. In the Copper Basin to the north are famed trout streams like the Big Lost River and Starhope Creek. Don't worry if you forgot to bring your flies. **Silver Creek Outfitters**, the Neiman-Marcus of fishing and hunting stores, offers more than 100,000 tied flies. It's located on Main Street in Ketchum and can provide guides and transportation. (208) 726-5282. For an easy day hike, drive 15 miles north of Ketchum on Idaho 75 to Baker Creek Road. Continue 9.6 miles on the dirt road, then take the steep but short 2.6-mile round-trip to Baker Lake. There's good trout fishing here. If you'd like to go mountain biking along cross-country trails that parallel the Wood River, you'll find it easy to arrange a rental at one of the local bike shops. In the evening you can enjoy outdoor concerts at Elkhorn Resort Lodge or, if you prefer, enjoy Sun Valley Resort's ice rink that's open year-round.

Tenth Day: Sun Valley to Jackson Hole (247 miles)

Take Idaho 75 south 27 miles to US 20. Drive east 45 miles to **Craters of the Moon National Monument**. This 83-square-mile area is a volcanic wonderland featuring lava cascades, tree molds, spatter cones, blast rocks, and other impressive geologic features. This weird landscape can be seen easily via a 7-mile loop drive. Stop at the visitor's center for an overview and route maps. Along the way you'll stop to enjoy some short walks to interesting features such as the **North Crater Flow, Devil's Orchard**, and **Inferno Cone**. Being careful to limit your hiking to paved trails, you'll have a chance to take the popular trail leading through lava tubes. The latter stop offers a chance to see the underground world of volcanic activity. Although this area has been geologically inactive since the time of Jesus, renewed activity is always a possibility. Visitor center hours are Thursday to Monday 8:00

a.m. to 6:00 p.m. mid-June to Labor Day. The rest of the
year hours are 8:00 a.m. to 4:30 p.m. (208) 527-3257.

Your extension to Montana and Idaho ends with a drive
across eastern Idaho. Begin by taking US 20 for 19 miles
to Arco at the Department of Energy's Idaho National
Engineering Laboratory. Twenty miles southeast on US 26
you'll reach the birthplace of nuclear-generated electrical
power. **EBR-1**, which opened in 1951, was also the site of
the first death at a nuclear plant when an exploding control rod impaled one of the operators on the reactor
dome. This site is also home to many other nuclear test
reactors operated by our government. It's not my idea of
a sightseeing highlight, but it is open for the curious from
8:00 a.m. to 4:00 p.m. in the summer and by appointment
the rest of the year. (208) 526-0050.

Continue east 47 miles to Idaho Falls on US 20. Then
take US 26 east 39 miles to Swan Valley. Here you pick up
Idaho 31 north 21 miles to Victor. Continue south on
Idaho 33 for 6 miles to the Wyoming line. Then drive 16
miles over Teton Pass to US 191 and Jackson. Spend the
night here (see Day 13 for lodging ideas) and drive north
33 miles the following morning to Moran Junction,
where you rejoin the main itinerary on Day 18.

YELLOWSTONE TO SOUTH PASS CITY

Today's itinerary takes you to one of the finest historic restorations in the Rockies, South Pass City. You'll drive down from Yellowstone along the foothills of the Wind River Range to this Oregon Trail landmark that was once the largest settlement between Denver and Salt Lake City. Along the way you'll visit the Wind River Indian Reservation and see the grave of Lewis and Clark's Indian guide, Sacajawea, and several missions. You'll also have a chance to visit Miner's Delight Inn in Atlantic City. Its restaurant attracts visitors from all over the West.

Suggested Schedule

7:00 a.m.	Depart Yellowstone National Park.
10:30 a.m.	Visit Wind River Indian Reservation at Fort Washakie.
2:00 p.m.	Tour South Pass City.
6:00 p.m.	Dinner at Miner's Delight Inn, Atlantic City.

Travel Route: Yellowstone National Park to South Pass City (227 miles)

Today's drive begins at Yellowstone's West Thumb Junction. Head south on US 191 for 45 miles to Moran Junction. Here, pick up US 287/26 southeast. The next 124 miles takes you back across the Continental Divide and along the Wind River to Fort Washakie. Continue south another 15 miles to Lander. Nine miles past Lander, take Wyoming 28 another 25 miles to South Pass City. You can spend the night in the South Pass City area or return to Lander. This paved two-lane route may have some heavy traffic in the Yellowstone Park area but is otherwise an easy trip. Beware of high winds as you go over mountain passes.

Sightseeing Highlights

▲▲**Wind River Indian Reservation**—Spread across more than two million acres, this Eastern Shoshone/ Northern Arapaho homeland was established in 1868. It is a popular jump-off point for expeditions into the Wind River Range. The reservation has five settlements, including two on today's route. One is Crowheart, located 85 miles east of Moran Junction. A sign on the north side of US 287 commemorates the spot where Shoshone and Bannock Indians vanquished the Crow tribe. Chief Washakie supposedly celebrated during the victory dance by tearing out the heart of the Crow chief and eating it.

The town of Fort Washakie is named for this popular Shoshone chief, who helped found the reservation and lived here until he died at age 102 in 1900. He was the first Indian chief to be buried with full military honors. While the reservation is best known for the beautiful mountains dominating its skyline, Fort Washakie is also a major Indian history hub and administrative headquarters of the Wind River Reservation. The tribal office is open weekdays from 8:00 a.m. to 4:45 p.m. (307) 332-3040. It's on US 287 16 miles north of Lander.

▲▲**Roberts Mission**—Located 1.5 miles southwest of Fort Washakie, this mission was founded by the Rev. John Roberts, who with his wife, Laura, devoted his life to the Shoshone children. Because the Indians had no written language, the Robertses set up a white man's school for the reservation. Today you can see the two-story red brick Shoshone School for Indian Girls built in 1889-90. Also here are a handsome log church, the Chapel of the Holy Saints John, and a small log cottage.

▲▲**Saint Michael's Mission**—Located in Ethete, 6 miles east of Fort Washakie, this Arapaho Episcopal Mission, like the Shoshone one, was founded by the Rev. John Roberts. Built around a circle between 1910 and 1917, the mission includes the log Church of Our Father's House, stone homes, a child care center, a post office, and a bead shop. Of special interest is St. Martha's cottage, a former staff house that now serves as the Arapaho Cultural and

Historical Center. This is an excellent place to learn about Arapaho traditions and see beautiful artifacts. This building, originally a residence for the school staff and children, displays Indian treasures, costumes, and scenes of milestones in tribal history.

▲▲▲ **Sacajawea Grave**—Visit the tribal cemetery located one mile northwest of the Shoshone Episcopal Mission. Here you'll find the grave of Sacajawea, the Indian guide who helped Lewis and Clark make their epic journey across the Rockies in 1804-1806. After assisting the explorers, she returned to her Indian tribe. The Shoshone believe she died on April 9, 1884, on the Wind River Reservation and was buried here by Reverend Roberts. This claim is disputed in North Dakota, where historians insist she died in their state at age 25. While they debate the details, you can enjoy a visit to this last resting place of one of America's authentic heroines.

▲▲▲ **South Pass City**—One of the great rewards of a trip through the Rockies is discovering an authentic piece of American pioneer history. This year, the 150th anniversary of the Oregon Trail, is an especially appropriate time to explore this famed route. A touchstone of the great westward migration route, South Pass is one of my favorite ghost towns, although that term seems like a misnomer. While only a few caretakers live in this nineteenth-century boomtown that was once home to 4,000, the community is experiencing a revival thanks to the dedicated restoration work of the state of Wyoming. Having survived armed conflict, epidemics, fires, unthinkable weather, vandalism, and a gold rush, this community in the Wind River Mountains is as rugged and remote today as it was more than a century ago.

The South Pass route pioneered across the Rockies by the Astorian fur trading party headed east in 1812 eventually became the main line west. Between 1840 and 1868, more than 500,000 emigrants crossed the Continental Divide via 7,550-foot-high South Pass. The discovery of gold in 1867 on local Willow Creek created an overnight boomtown, and South Pass flourished until about 1872.

Today the city is one of the largest historical restora-

tions in the Rockies and definitely one of the best.
Twenty-five restored buildings, including storefronts,
cabins, saloon, hotel, stamp mill, school, jail, livery stable, and ice house, capture this grand era. On your tour
you'll see approximately thirty period room exhibits and
the visitors center and have a chance to hike the local
nature trails. One of the town's most popular attractions
is the Smith-Sherlock General Store, where you'll find an
old-fashioned coffee grinder, a butter churn, and an
antique scale as well as shelves full of nineteenth-century
artifacts. Of special interest is the home of Esther Morris,
who became the nation's first female justice of the peace
here in 1870. Roam the area around South Pass and you'll
find old mining buildings, stamp mills, headframes, and
artifacts. The historic site is open daily 9:00 a.m. to 6:00
p.m. from May 15 to October 15. Admission is free. Living
history programs and lectures are exhibited during the
summer months, and there's a major Fourth of July
celebration. Fishermen will enjoy trying the excellent
streams and small lakes in this area. Check with the visitor center, (307) 332-3684.

Atlantic City, South Pass's sister city a few miles to the
north, is the home of Miner's Delight Inn, a delightful restaurant serving fixed price dinners, as well as breakfasts,
Wednesday through Sunday. Reservations are required.
Stop by the Atlantic City Mercantile and you'll see the
100-year-old bar. (307) 332-5143. Another Atlantic City
landmark is St. Andrew's Episcopal Church, which still
has many of the original furnishings. In the hills above
the town you'll find more historic mining structures.

Always exercise caution when exploring mining ruins,
and be sure to keep your children close to you. You can
never be too careful around these old buildings and
shafts. Also be sure to watch your kids around the fast-
running streams in this area.

Lodging
The **Miner's Delight Inn** in Atlantic City, (307)
332-3513, has a few rooms and modest cabins available in

the summer months. Rates start around $50. Lander, 34 miles north of South Pass City, offers lodging for $26 to $55 at the **Budget Host Pronghorn Lodge**, 150 E. Main Street, (307) 332-3940. In the same price range is the **Maverick** at 808 Main Street, (307) 332-2821. Another choice is the **Silver Spur** at 340 N. 10th Street, (307) 332-5189. **McDougall Bed and Breakfast** is at 871 Garfield Street, (307) 332-3392. Rates run under $50. Another possibility is **Black Mountain Ranch** on the North Fork of the Popo Agie River near Lander. Call (307) 332-6442 for details.

Two improved campgrounds are available 25 miles south of Lander via Wyoming Highway 28. They are the **Atlantic City Campground** on Atlantic City Road and **Big Atlantic Gulch** on Miner's Delight Road. Both these Bureau of Land Management facilities north of Atlantic City are open May 1 to October 31. For details, ask at the South Pass visitor information center. Units are $3.

Food
In addition to the **Miner's Delight** in Atlantic City, you can dine informally at the **Mercantile,** which serves steaks and burgers, located on Wyoming Highway 28, ¾-mile west of the South Pass turnoff. In Lander, first choice for breakfast is the **Commons Restaurant** at 170 E. Main Street, (307) 332-5149. Also recommended is the **Hitching Rock** on Wyoming 28/287 on the south side of Lander, (307) 332-4322. Try the steaks.

Itinerary Options
Here are three intriguing possibilities for travelers with extra time.

Sinks Canyon State Park: Located 6 miles southwest of Lander on Wyoming 131, you'll find this interesting geologic anomaly. Here the Popo Agie River disappears into a cavern and then reappears half a mile later in a beautiful pool. A visitor center offers background on the canyon and has information on the Popo Agie and Nature Trails walks. Allow one to two hours for your visit. There's also a campground.

To see the red rock **Wind River Canyon**, one of the
great geologic treasures of the Rockies, drive 25 miles
northeast from Lander to Riverton and pick up US 26
another 22 miles north to Shoshone. Twelve miles north
on US 20 you'll enter Wind River Canyon. Over the centuries this stream has carved a 2,000-foot-deep channel
between the Owl Creek and Bridger mountains. A history
book carved in stone, the strata tell the story of this
region back through the millennia. The Wyoming Geological Association has thoughtfully erected signs along
the 16-mile canyon which link these formations with
periods ranging from the Precambrian to the Mesozoic.
At the north end of the canyon, the Wind River becomes
the Big Horn River, which explains why this spot is called
the Wedding of the Waters.

Four miles beyond the canyon mouth is Thermopolis,
home of **Hot Springs State Park**, where you can bathe
year-round in the waters of the largest mineral hot spring
in the world. A herd of buffalo is also in the park for your
viewing pleasure. After overnighting in Thermopolis,
retrace your route to Lander and rejoin the main itinerary.

SOUTH PASS CITY TO SARATOGA

Today's itinerary takes you south to the Medicine Bow National Forest and Wyoming's Sierra Madre range. You'll have a chance to see another first-class historic restoration in Encampment and go for a dip in Saratoga Hot Springs. Also on today's itinerary are Oregon Trail landmarks and a chance to fish one of the best streams in the Rockies.

Suggested Schedule	
8:00 a.m.	Depart South Pass City.
9:30 a.m.	Arrive Split Rock/Oregon Trail
12:30 p.m.	Arrive at Encampment. Picnic lunch.
1:00 p.m.	Visit Grand Encampment Museum.
3:00 p.m.	Return to Saratoga.
Balance of day	Hike, bike, fish, swim, or loaf.

Travel Route: South Pass City to Encampment (192 miles)

Take Wyoming 28 north 25 miles. Pick up US 287 for another 73 miles southeast through the Green Mountains to Muddy Gap. Continue south on US 287 another 44 miles to Rawlins. Pick up I-80 for 21 miles east to Walcott. Take US 130 south 38 miles to Riverside. Continue south one mile on Wyoming 70 to Encampment. Then double back 19 miles to Saratoga, where you'll spend the night. These are all good highways and, with the exception of I-80, should have light traffic. RV drivers and those pulling trailers should beware of high winds.

Sightseeing Highlights

▲ **Split Rock**—Located 13 miles east of Jeffrey City on US 287, this Sweetwater River Valley landmark was once a causeway used by buffalo, Indians, and finally emigrants headed west on the Oregon Trail. Split at its summit, the rock was a major landmark for travelers bound for the promised land. The area's history is explained at a highway turnout south of the promontory.

▲ **Whiskey Gap**—Just south of Muddy Gap as you head toward Lamont on US 287, you'll pass Whiskey Gap. This was the site of the historic 1862 prohibition raid on a big wagon train full of whiskey. In the search-and-destroy mission, the cavalry ended up irrigating this hardscrabble land with 80-proof spirits.

▲▲ **Grand Encampment Museum**—Like South Pass City, the museum at 7th and Barnett in the town of Encampment is a historic restoration you won't want to miss. This copper boomtown was created at the end of the nineteenth century thanks to a copper strike in the local Sierra Madre. Ore mined here was shipped back across the Continental Divide to an Encampment smelter via a 16-mile-long aerial tramway. It took 375 wooden towers to support the conveyor, and today you'll find three of them, along with thirteen period buildings, at the museum. Old ghost town structures, a 65-foot fire tower, cabins, a barn, a bakery, a blacksmith shop, and a stage station with a sod roof and outhouse are all part of the fun. In addition, the museum features Indian artifacts, buggies, nineteenth-century clothing, historic photos, furniture, and even pioneer poetry. The museum is open from 1:00 p.m. to 5:00 p.m. from Memorial Day to Labor Day and the same hours on Saturday and Sunday from Labor Day though October. It's open by appointment at other times. (307) 327-5308.

▲▲ **Saratoga**—This town is best known for the clear and odorless waters of Saratoga Hot Springs, open to the public at no charge. The Saratoga Historical and Cultural Center at the Union Pacific rail station on Wyoming 130 has good exhibits on the Native American and pioneer history of the Platte Valley region. It's open 1:00 p.m. to 5:00 p.m. Memorial Day to Labor Day and by appointment the rest of the year. (307) 326-5511. Great Rocky Mountain Outfitters at 216 E. Walnut Street offers half-day float trips ($20) and fishing trips on the North Platte. (307) 326-8750. The 70-mile stream between Saratoga and the Colorado line is one of the state's most scenic. Fishermen take note: this section of the North Platte is excellent. If you have extra time, Wyoming 130 to the east offers a dra-

matic paved route across the Medicine Bow Range to the
village of Centennial. You'll enjoy great views of the
snowy 12,000-foot peaks and probably be able to spot
elk and mule deer and possibly a bobcat or two. Be sure
to always keep your distance from the wildlife. The backcountry of the 1.6-million-acre Medicine Bow National
Forest has numerous streams and lakes ideal for trout
fishing and bird-watching. For more information, call the
Medicine Bow National Forest office at (307) 745-8971.

Lodging
In Saratoga, rooms at the historic **Wolf Hotel**, 101 E.
Bridge Street, start at $35. (307) 326-5525. The **Saratoga
Inn** on East Pick Pike Road, which has a golf course and
pool, charges $50 and up. The inn also has RV sites at $14
per night. (307) 326-5261. Another possibility is the $40 a
night **Hood House Bed and Breakfast** at 214 N. Third
Street. (307) 326-8901. For a fee, Hood House patrons can
fish at Cedar Creek Ranch on a 2-mile North Platte stretch
or in their choice of three reservoirs. In Encampment,
Lorraine's Bed and Breakfast is located at 1016 Lomax
Street. Rooms run $38. (307) 327-5200. Hiking, float
trips, fishing, golfing, swimming, and rock hunting are all
convenient to this establishment.

Campers can stay at **Saratoga Lake Ranch RV Park**
one mile north of Saratoga. It offers basic tent and trailer
sites for $5 and up. In Riverside, the **Lazy Acres RV Park
and Campground** at the Wyoming 230 Bridge offers
excellent facilities for $5 and up. (307) 327-5968.

Food
The Hotel Wolf Restaurant at 101 E. Bridge Street in
Saratoga is a good bet for steaks. (307) 326-5525. For family dining, try **Mom's Kitchen** at 402 South First Street,
(307) 326-5136. **Wally's Pizza** is at 110 E. Bridge Street,
(307) 326-8472. In Encampment, the **Oasis** at 706
Rankin Street has a dining room, coffee shop, soda fountain, and game room. (307) 327-5129.

Itinerary Option: Independence Rock
A key landmark on the Oregon Trail route is Independence Rock, 24 miles east of Muddy Gap on Wyoming

220. This outcropping was a popular place for Oregon Trail travelers to paint or carve their names. Due to a shortage of space, some travelers climbed as high as 80 feet to find a piece of the rock big enough to accommodate their John Hancocks. Those who were in a hurry could pay Mormons—some of whom charged as much as $5 for the service—to carve their names. Historian Gregory Franzwa, author of the definitive *The Oregon Trail Revisited* (St. Louis: Patrice Press, 1988), points out that every famous name connected with the Oregon Trail is or was recorded here. Among them is Lansford Hastings, the man who went on to pioneer the Hastings cutoff from the main trail. Hastings and his partner were seized by the Sioux while carving their names and were later traded back to the Donner caravan for a little tobacco. If only the Sioux had held on to these men, the Donners might have stuck to the main line and survived. Instead, the Donner party took his route advice and was hopelessly delayed and caught in a fatal Sierra snowstorm. About five miles west of Independence Rock, you'll be able to spot (from Wyoming 220) a small gash in the ridge. This spot, five miles distant, is Devils Gate, a handsome cut in the ridge made by the Sweetwater River. This was a major landmark on the Oregon Trail and impassable by anyone without climbing gear. Since it's on private land, you must see it from Wyoming 220.

Wyoming Frontier Prison—Located at 5th and Walnut in Rawlins, this Romanesque territorial prison offers a tour of the old cell blocks, clinic, gallows, and gas chamber. A museum tells the story of outlaws like the great train robber Bill Carlisle, who did time here. Nine inmates were hung in this prison. Closed in 1981, the prison now offers hour-long walking tours every half hour from 8:30 a.m. to 5:30 p.m. daily from Memorial Day to Labor Day. There are also special 9:30 p.m. tours on Wednesday, Friday, and Saturday. Call for an appointment the rest of the year. Admission is $3 for adults, $2.50 for seniors and children ages 6 to 18. (307) 324-4111.

DAY 20

SARATOGA TO ROCKY MOUNTAIN NATIONAL PARK

After a relaxed morning in Saratoga, head south to the last of the four national parks on this itinerary. Here you'll see Grand Lake, make your final crossing of the Continental Divide, and have a chance to hike part of the Colorado River Trail.

Suggested Schedule

9:00 a.m.	Depart for Rocky Mountain National Park.
11:30 a.m.	Arrive Grand Lake.
1:00 p.m.	Visit Kauffman House.
2:00 p.m.	Hike the Colorado River Trail or take a boat tour of Grand Lake.
6:00 p.m.	Dinner at Grand Lake Lodge.
Evening	At leisure.

Travel Route: Saratoga to Grand Lake (122 miles)
Take Wyoming 130 south 18 miles to Riverside and continue another 27 miles on Wyoming 230 south to the Colorado line. Continue 77 miles south on Colorado 125 over Willow Creek Pass (9,600 feet) to US 40. Go east 3 miles to Granby and pick up US 34 north 14 miles to Grand Lake. This route is a good mountain road with light traffic until you hit the last few miles into Rocky Mountain National Park.

Sightseeing Highlights
▲▲▲ **Grand Lake**—This, your gateway to Rocky Mountain National Park, is the state's largest natural lake. Located at 8,300 feet, it offers more than 150 miles of shoreline and connects with Shadow Mountain Lake. The lake area is an excellent spot for hiking, riding, swimming, and boating and offers rafting trips, golfing, and a chance to spot wildlife including deer, bighorn sheep, beaver, and elk. Grand Lake Village offers museums, summer stock theater, and a wide range of resorts and restaurants.

▲ **Kauffman House**—Built in 1892, this log home at 407 Pitkin has been restored into a fine pioneer museum.

Exhibits offer an intriguing look at early-day life in this
region. It's open 1:00 to 5:00 p.m. June through
August and by appointment at other times. (303) 627-8562.

▲▲▲ **Rocky Mountain National Park**—Drive into this
265,000-acre park to sample one of its fine hiking trails.
Beginning in the Front Range and sweeping across the
Continental Divide, Rocky Mountain National Park has 59
peaks over 12,000 feet, including 14,255-foot-high Longs
Peak. Home to the Indians for nearly 15,000 years, this
region was occupied by the Cheyenne, Arapaho, Ute, and
Shoshone when the white man first arrived in the nineteenth century. Famous for its beautiful peaks and canyons,
the park offers a wide array of trails and highways that
showcase this alpine terrain. Many U-shaped valleys
formed by glacial advances offer spectacular hiking
opportunities. For example, the trail to Glacier Gorge,
Mills Lake, and Jewel Lake offers some of the best hiking
in the Colorado Rockies. While this park has many of the
amenities you've been enjoying for nearly three weeks, it
also has a number of unique assets. They include Trail
Ridge Road, surely one of the nation's great mountain
drives, the living history exhibits of the Never Summer
Ranch, and, for the handicapped, the Five Sense Trail
around Sprague Lake created by the Youth Conservation
Corps. As you explore Rocky Mountain National Park, I
think you'll find that it's the appropriate finale to your
22-day odyssey. From Fall River Pass or the Stanley Hotel
to a hike into Thunder Lake, the region in and around the
park is full of grand surprises.

The Colorado River Trail is a great place to begin your
exploration. Drive north from Grand Lake 8 miles on US
34 to the Timber Lake trailhead and park. Here you can
take the easy 4-mile round-trip hike to Shipler Park. If
you have extra time tomorrow, you could take the longer
8-mile round-trip hike up to the old mining town of Lulu
City. Allow half a day for the latter trip. For information
on these and other park opportunities, call (303) 586-2371.

An alternative is a narrated boat trip on Grand Lake.
You can ride with Whale Watch Tour, which guarantees
you'll see no cetaceans on your 45 minute trip. There are
four daily departures in the summer from the Spirit Lake

Marina at 1244 Lake Avenue. Rentals are also available. (303) 627-8158. Bring along a jacket or warm sweater.

Lodging

Grand Lake Lodge offers cabins for around $40 to $90 in a beautiful setting. (303) 627-3967. For reservations off-season, call (303) 759-5848. **Lemmon Lodge** on Grand Lake is a rustic spot with the best miniature golf course in the region. Rooms are $45 to $165. (303) 627-3314. **Driftwood Lodge** offers rooms from $36 to $71. It's located at 12255 US 34 adjacent to Shadow Lake. (303) 627-3654. The **Rapids Lodge**, which also offers cabins and condos, is at 209 Rapids Lane. (303) 627-3707. Rates run $45 to $120.

Camping is available at **Timber Creek Campground**, 7 miles north of the Rocky Mountain National Park entrance on Colorado 34. Unreserved sites are fully equipped. **Winding River Resort** offers ranch camping on a 160-acre site. Horseback riding, fishing, hayrides, ice cream socials, and evening movies are all part of the fun. Take US 34 one mile north of Grand Lake and then turn left 1.5 miles. Full hookups are available. (303) 627-3215. Bed and breakfast is also available for those who don't want to rough it. Rates run $55 to $80.

For additional lodging information, call the **Grand Lake Chamber of Commerce** at (303) 627-3402 or stop by their office at Grand Avenue and West Portal Road. Remember that many establishments in this region operate on a seasonal basis, closing at the end of summer.

Food

Grand Lake Lodge offers a terrific view of the lake. It's a great place for dinner, a drink, and a chance to watch the sunset. This beautiful pine lodge is located off US 34, a quarter mile north of the turnoff to Grand Lake. (303) 627-3967. Upscale Italian dining can be found in Grand Lake at the **Rapids Restaurant**, 209 Rapids Lane, (303) 627-3707. For family dining, try the **Corner Cupboard Inn** at 1028 Grand Avenue, (303) 627-3813. Family-style dining is recommended at the **Mountain Inn**, 612 Grand Avenue, (303) 627-3385. For breakfast, go to the **Chuck Hole Cafe** at 1119 Grand Avenue, (303) 627-3509.

ROCKY MOUNTAIN NATIONAL PARK

Today you'll take Trail Ridge Road across the park, pausing to visit historic Never Summer Ranch before continuing to Glacier Gorge Junction, where you'll hike to Mills and Jewel lakes. In the evening you'll have a chance to enjoy the beauty of the park region from the veranda of the historic Stanley Hotel.

Suggested Schedule

8:00 a.m.	Depart on Trail Ridge Road.
8:15 a.m.	Visit Never Summer Ranch.
9:15 a.m.	Resume Trail Ridge Road.
10:15 a.m.	Alpine Visitors Center.
1:00 p.m.	Arrive Glacier Gorge Junction. Lunch.
1:30 p.m.	Hike to Mills Lake and Jewel Lake.
5:30 p.m.	Check into your campground or lodge on the east side of the park or in the Estes Park area.
Evening	Visit Stanley Hotel.

Travel Route: Across Rocky Mountain National Park (50 miles)
Take US 34 north to the Never Summer Ranch turnoff. Continue along Trail Ridge Road, pausing at the Alpine Visitors Center to learn more about the high country. Then continue your drive through mountain meadows and valleys to Bear Lake Road. Here, take the shuttle bus to Glacier Gorge Junction, then return to park headquarters and your hotel or campground. In the evening, take US 34 into Estes Park to visit the Stanley Hotel at 333 Wonderview.

Sightseeing Highlights
▲▲ **Never Summer Ranch**—This former dude ranch is now a living history museum. Spread across 800 acres in the Kawuneeche Valley, the early twentieth-century ranch complex is an excellent way to enjoy a look at

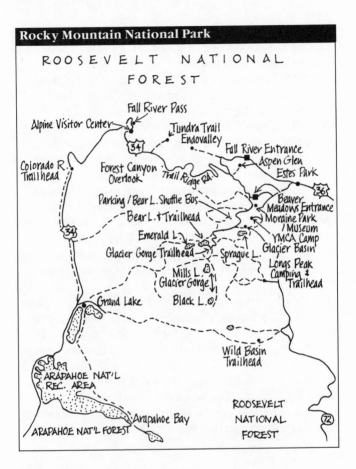

Rocky Mountain National Park

homestead life in the Rockies. It is open for tours via a one-mile-long trail. You can also explore the surrounding wilderness and enjoy the beaver ponds. Free.

▲ **Trail Ridge Road**—As it climbs up to the 12,183-foot level, Trail Ridge Road offers a panoramic overview of the park's alpine terrain. From Grand Lake, head up into the Kawuneeche Valley, across the Continental Divide and Fall River Pass. More than 11 miles of this route are above timberline, where you'll see alpine tundra, meadows full of wildflowers, and beautiful streams and lakes. Here, on the roof of the Rockies, glacial peaks surround your route. As you continue driving along this winding route paralleling an old Indian trail, you'll want to get out periodically to explore some of the picturesque meadows and trails. A good place to get an overview is the Alpine Visitors Center near the route's summit. Inside you can see exhibits on the local tundra landscape and pick up hiking maps. After leaving the Alpine Visitors Center, drive down to the half-hour-long tundra trail.

▲▲▲ Hike to Mills Lake and Jewel Lake—Departing from Glacier Gorge Junction, this 6-mile hike on the park's east side is today's highlight. It's easy to exhaust superlatives in the Rockies, but this walk, which gains 700 feet in elevation, proves once again that the Rockies are a continual source of inspiration. Carved out by a great ice river, this glacial basin is one of the park's gems. If the winds are right, you may even hear musical sounds as you walk through the gorge region. Along the trail you'll see a number of small glaciers at the head of the valley.

▲ Stanley Hotel—Built in 1909 by F. O. Stanley, creator of the Stanley Steamer, a pioneer car, the Stanley is perhaps best known for its supporting role in the film version of Stephen King's *The Shining*. This national historic landmark, which features a prototype of Stanley's vehicle in the lobby, has been beautifully renovated, and the veranda offers great views of the Estes Park area. Come for a drink. There may be an evening concert, the perfect way to wind up your last night in the mountains.

Itinerary Option

The half-mile-long Sprague Lake Five Senses Trail is wheelchair accessible. If you have extra time and would like to try an uncrowded trail, consider the 12-mile round-trip hike from Endovalley Road to Lawn Lake. You'll walk along the Roaring River drainage, ascending gradually into the Mummy Range. Great views. Allow all day.

Lodging

First choice is **YMCA Camp of the Rockies**, which is open to the general public. Take US 36 west to Colorado 66 south to the camp turnoff. If you have kids, this complex with horseback riding, miniature golf, whitewater rafting, roller skating, and swimming is a must. You'll be tempted to extend your stay to take advantage of all the opportunities on this 1,400-acre site. There are 500 lodge rooms and more than 200 cabins equipped as housekeeping units. (303) 586-3341. Rooms are $42 to $182. The **Stanley Hotel** at 333 Wonderview offers rooms from $80 to $120. (303) 586-3371 or (800) ROCKIES. **Streamside Cabins** at 1260 Fall River Road offers pleasant riverfront cottages ranging from $105 to $175. (303) 586-6464. **Trapper's Motor Inn** at 553 West Elkhorn has housekeeping units for $39 to $58. (303) 586-2833. **The Riversong Bed and Breakfast** offers rooms for $80 to $160. It's located on the Big Thompson River. (303) 586-4666. For other lodging possibilities, your best bet is to call the Estes Park Referral Service at (800) 44-ESTES.

Camping is available on the east side of Rocky Mountain National Park at Moraine Park, Longs Peak, Aspenglen, and Glacier Basin campgrounds. You can reserve dates between May 31 and September 7 at Glacier Basin and Moraine Park through Mistix, (800) 365-2267. All other sites are on a first-come, first-served basis. Camping is limited to seven days in the summer, three days at Longs Peak. Summer fees are $9 a night, while off-season fees are $6. Sanitary dump stations are available at Moraine Park and Glacier Basin. There are no showers in the park campgrounds. **Estes Park Campground**, 5 miles southwest of Estes Park on Colorado 66, has all the usual facilities, $9 and up, no RV hookups. (303) 586-4188. **Spruce Lake RV Park** at 1050 Mary's Lake Road has complete facilities and good fishing at $16.95 and up. Go 1.25 miles west on US 36, then one-eighth mile south on Mary's Lake Road. (303) 586-2889.

Food

In Estes Park, the inexpensive **La Casa Del Estorito** at 222 E. Elkhorn Avenue offers Mexican and Cajun dining in a garden setting. (303) 586-2807. At sunset, try the moderately priced **Sundeck** restaurant at 915 South

Moraine. It has great views of the Rockies. Enjoy the
trout. (303) 586-9832. The **Dark Horse** at Fawn Valley
Inn, 2760 Fall River Road, specializes in continental
cuisine. (303) 586-5654. **Orlando's** at The Wheel Bar,
132 East Elkhorn, is a good steakhouse. (303) 586-9381.
The moderately priced **Other Side Restaurant** at 900
Moraine Avenue is good for families. (303) 586-2171.
Barleen Family Country Music Dinner Theater, one
mile south of town on Colorado 7, serves roast beef dinners. Shows start at 7:00 p.m. (303) 586-5749.

ROCKY MOUNTAIN NATIONAL PARK TO BOULDER AND DENVER

Descend the Rockies via the dramatic Peak to Peak Highway and Boulder Canyon. After pausing for a walk along the creek at Boulder Falls, visit Colorado's leading college town, enjoying street life on the mall, a historic Victorian neighborhood, and the university planetarium, before returning to Denver.

Suggested Schedule

9:00 a.m.	Depart Rocky Mountain National Park via Peak to Peak Highway.
11:00 a.m.	Boulder Falls.
1:00 p.m.	Lunch on the Boulder Mall.
2:00 p.m.	Explore Boulder Mall.

Balance of afternoon at leisure.
Return to Denver.

Travel Route: Estes Park to Denver via Boulder (104 miles)

Take Colorado 7 and Colorado 72 south 41 miles to Nederland. Continue east 16 miles to Boulder. Entering the city via Canyon Boulevard, park downtown in the vicinity of South Broadway and walk north two blocks to the Pearl Street Mall. Return to Denver via US 36.

Boulder

One of the best-known college towns in the Rockies, Boulder is home of the Colorado Music Festival, the Colorado Shakespeare Festival, the José Cuervo Doubles Volleyball Tournament, and the Kinetic Fest, featuring land- and water-worthy human-powered sculpture. The town's intellectual hub, the University of Colorado, offers a wide array of special summer events including music, dance and arts, theater, and film programs. Here on the edge of the Front Range you can visit the I. M. Pei-

designed National Center for Atmospheric Research,
which offers self-guided tours Monday through Friday
from 8:00 a.m. to 5:00 p.m. and on Saturday, Sunday, and
holidays from 9:00 a.m. to 3:00 p.m. (303) 497-1174. Free.
You can also tour the anthropology and paleontology
exhibits at the University of Colorado's Henderson
Museum at 15th Street and Broadway on the campus. It's
open Monday through Friday 9:00 a.m. to 5:00 p.m.,
Saturday 9:00 a.m. to 4:00 p.m., and Sunday 10:00 a.m. to
4:00 p.m. (303) 492-6892. Free.

This university was the first school in the United States
to have its own satellite in orbit around the earth. While
it's hard to get permission to tour the computer facility
where the satellite data are processed, you can space out
in other ways at the university's Fiske Planetarium, which
has one of the largest, most detailed, and most optically
precise star projectors anywhere. Besides educational
presentations on astronomy, the planetarium augments
its budget with rock music shows featuring lasers and
outstanding special effects. Located on the campus's
Regent Drive, the planetarium is open Monday through
Friday 8:00 a.m. to 12:00 noon and 1:00 p.m. to 5:00 p.m.
The student union cafeteria is named for Lake City's
alleged cannibal, Alferd Packer (see Day 6; and yes, that
really is the correct spelling of his first name). With its
sculpture park, kids' fishing ponds, historic Boulderado
Hotel, and flourishing arts scene, Boulder is a good place
to wind up your days in the Rockies.

Sightseeing Highlights
▲▲ **Peak to Peak Highway**—Linking Estes Park with
Central City, Colorado 7 and Colorado 72 take you
through mountain towns like Meeker Park, Allenspark,
Raymond, and Ward. This sometimes windy route
through the Roosevelt National Forest is an ideal way to
sample some of the old silver, gold, and tungsten camps
that helped colonize the region. There are ghost towns
like Caribou and hiking opportunities in the Indian Peaks
area. The latter is reached by heading west 5.2 miles from

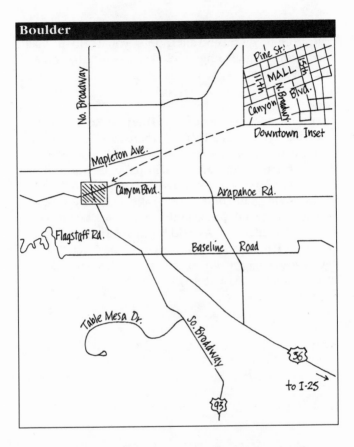

Ward on County Road 112. A network of hiking trails leads up to many alpine lakes. There's also a campground and a picnic area.

▲▲ **Boulder Falls**—The highlight of Boulder Canyon, this cascade is your last stop in the Rockies. Enjoy a walk along Boulder Creek. On the way you may see rock climbers scaling the canyon walls.

▲▲ **Pearl Street Mall**—From the chic to the offbeat, Boulder's downtown mall is a great place for people-watching and shopping. Blessed with sculptures, fountains, and flower beds, the mall is a good place to shop for street art and a last-minute souvenir. It's also a popular

venue for street performers. During the summer, especially on sunny weekend afternoons, you'll find the mall
lined with bluegrass singers, clowns, mimes, and sometimes even acrobats.

Food

Just off the mall, go native at the **Harvest Restaurant
and Bakery**, 1738 Pearl Street, where you'll enjoy natural foods at moderate prices. (303) 449-6223. **Pour La
France** offers coffee and pastries on the patio at 1001
Pearl Street. (303) 449-3929. **Dot's Diner** at 799 Pearl
Street also has patio dining. (303) 449-1323. If you're
looking for the ultimate Boulder view, take Baseline Road
west to Flagstaff Road. Ascend Flagstaff Mountain to the
Flagstaff House restaurant with its 10-tier deck. If
you're going to have dinner in Boulder, this is the ideal
sunset choice. (303) 442-4640.

COLORADO SPRINGS AREA

The state's second-largest city, Colorado Springs, seems to be perched literally on the brink of infinity. Where else can you look out at spacious skies from the summit of Pikes Peak and also contemplate Armageddon from the bowels of our nation's nuclear air command post? Blessed with one of the region's grand hotels, a fine zoo, first-rate caving, and the picturesque rock formations in the Garden of the Gods, this city is a popular resort choice and a natural extension to our itinerary. Easily reached via a dramatic backcountry road is the historic Cripple Creek mining district. Also an important part of any tour to this region is a trip to the famed Royal Gorge area, where you can raft the Grand Canyon of the Arkansas River.

First Day: Colorado Springs

Head south 70 miles from Denver to Colorado Springs on Interstate 25. Exit at Circle Drive (exit 138) and head west. Circle Drive turns into Lake Avenue and leads you to the front of the **Broadmoor Hotel**. This Italian Renaissance building was one of the most elegant resort hotels in the nation when it was built in 1914 at a cost exceeding $80 million. Spencer Penrose, who built the hotel, made his fortune in Cripple Creek not by finding gold but by opening a realty office to sell mining claims, then establishing refineries where his customers brought the ore after digging it out of the ground. The Broadmoor was originally a gambling casino (now the golf clubhouse). The main part of the hotel has retained its Roaring Twenties ambience, while a larger modern annex has been built on the far side of the lake.

After visiting the Broadmoor, see the **Cheyenne Mountain Zoo**, the nation's only mountain zoo. It's located on Mirada Road southwest of the Broadmoor, midway up Cheyenne Mountain. The zoo got its start when visiting foreign dignitaries gave Spencer Penrose a

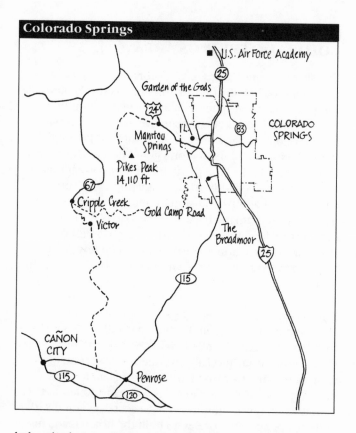

Colorado Springs

U.S. Air Force Academy

25

Garden of the Gods

24

COLORADO
SPRINGS

83

Manitou
Springs

Pikes Peak
14,110 ft.

67

Cripple Creek

Gold Camp Road

Victor

The
Broadmoor

25

115

CAÑON
CITY

115

Penrose

120

baby elephant and a matched pair of leopards. Feeling
that these hazards might make golf a little too challenging, Penrose built this beautiful mountainside zoo. Open
summer 9:00 a.m. to 5:00 p.m. and winter 9:00 a.m. to
4:00 p.m. Adults $5.50, seniors $4, and children ages 3 to
11 $3. (719) 475-9555.

Two miles above the zoo on a paved switchback road is
the **Will Rogers Shrine of the Sun**. Spencer Penrose
had already begun construction of this fabulously located
stone tower as a memorial and final resting place for himself and his wife (they are buried in the small chapel in
the base of the tower). When his friend, humorist Will
Rogers, died in a plane crash in Alaska, Penrose dedicated

the shrine to his memory and so became the only man in history to make a tourist attraction out of his own grave.

Next, return to 21st Street north and US 24 and Manitou Avenue west to Ruxton Avenue. This route leads to the **Manitou and Pikes Peak Cog Railway**, which begins in Manitou Springs. Over 100,000 people each summer drive their cars up the Pikes Peak Highway, 19 miles from the entrance gate above the town of Cascade on west US 24 to the summit house. The unpaved portion of the road is also the course of the Pikes Peak Hill Climb auto race, held annually in early July. Only the first 7 miles are paved; the first 2 miles and the 3 miles of switchbacks above Glen Cove Inn are steep and scary, and the last 4 miles are high enough in elevation to make some vehicles run poorly. Avoid the aggravation and possibility of breakdowns or brake problems on this difficult road by taking the Pikes Peak Cog Railway from Manitou Springs instead. The cog train goes up the opposite side of the mountain from the road. It climbs 7,359 feet to the top of the 14,110-foot-high summit. From the top, you can see Denver and the Sangre de Cristo Mountains. Open 8:00 a.m. to 5:20 p.m. daily from May to October. Trips leave every 80 minutes; they take 3 hours and 15 minutes. (719) 685-5401. The fare is $20.50 for adults and $9 for children.

Where to Eat: The longtime favorite Colorado Springs restaurant for lunch or dinner is **Giuseppe's**, by the railroad tracks down the hill behind the Antlers Doubletree Hotel downtown. Giuseppe's was already a popular local pizza and beer hangout in another location before it moved to the renovated former railroad passenger depot. While it now also serves such entrées as steak and snow crab, the specialties at this inexpensive to moderate restaurant continue to be great pizzas and huge sandwiches. (719) 635-3111. The **Sunbird Restaurant** at 230 Point of the Pines Drive has an inviting patio restaurant with the best views in town. (719) 599-8550. For Mexican food, try **Señor Manuel's** at 4660 N. Nevada Street, (719) 598-3033. The **Mission Inn** at 6799 N. Academy Boulevard also has good Mexican fare, (719) 598-3107.

Michelle's at 122 North Tejon is famous for its homemade ice cream sundaes and candy. (719) 633-5089.
    Where to Stay: If price is no object, the **Broadmoor**,
offering rooms for $120 to $240, is a good lodging choice
with beautiful grounds, a golf course, and close proximity to the zoo. This resort is at 1 Lake Avenue. (800)
634-7711. The **Antlers Doubletree Hotel** is a good
choice. Rooms start around $80. (719) 473-5600. **The
Villa Motel** 481 Manitou Avenue in M Mitououprings
offers rooms for $48 to $80. (719) 685-5492. For bed and
breakfast, try **On A Ledge** at 336 El Paso Boulevard in
Manitou Springs. Rooms run $70 to $110. (719) 685-4265.
Another B&B, **The Holden House** at 1102 W. Pikes Peak
Avenue in Colorado Springs, has rooms for $57 to $85.
(719) 471-3980. The rooms are all named for mining
towns. **The Garden of the Gods Campground** at 3704
W. Colorado Avenue has full amenities as well as a heated
pool, an entertainment pavilion, barbecues, and ice
cream socials. Sites run $16 to $20. (800) 345-8197 or
(719) 475-9450. Similar units at the Peak View Campground, 4954 North Nevada Avenue, run $10 to $16. (719)
598-1434.

**Second Day: Garden of the Gods and Manitou
Springs**
Begin at the **Garden of the Gods**, a national landmark at
1401 Recreation Way, (719) 578-6640. The red sandstone
rocks and pinnacles are a great spot to begin your day
with a morning hike. Return to US 24 and head west a
short distance to the turnoff (north) for the **Cave of the
Winds**. Here you can tour dramatically lit caverns and
rock formations. The cave is located north of US 24
above Manitou Springs and is open 9:00 a.m. to 9:00 p.m.
daily in summer and 10:00 a.m. to 5:00 p.m. daily in winter. Admission for adults is $8, for children $4. (719)
685-5444. Then take the one-way Williams Canyon Road
to return to Manitou Avenue, the main street of Manitou
Springs, a onetime spa with beautiful Victorians along its
tree-lined streets.
    Twenty years before the founding of Colorado Springs,

this town was a popular tourist destination thanks to its curative waters (in fact, there are no springs in Colorado Springs; the city was named for its proximity to Manitou Springs). Most of the eighty springs in Manitou Springs have now been capped. The town's best-known mansion, 28-room **Miramont Castle** at 9 Capitol Hill Avenue, is open for tours in summer from 10:00 a.m. to 5:00 p.m.; Labor Day to Thanksgiving and January to March, 1:00 p.m. to 3:00 p.m.; and March to Memorial Day, 11:00 a.m. to 3:00 p.m. (719) 685-1011. Admission is $2.50 for adults, $1 for children.

Seven Falls in South Cheyenne Canyon is a venerable but very commercialized tourist attraction. You can see comparable scenery for free in **North Cheyenne Canyon**, a municipal mountain park. Take US 24 east to Colorado Springs and turn south on 21st Street and take either Cheyenne Boulevard or Cheyenne Road west (they merge). Past Helen Hunt Falls at the upper end of the canyon, the paved road climbs up to join the unpaved Gold Camp Road, a 30-mile-long trip that takes at least two hours to reach your destination, the historic **Cripple Creek Mining District**. The rugged, steep ride, not recommended for large RVs or vehicles towing trailers, begins east of Manitou Springs and follows an old rail bed through beautiful backcountry. Along the way you'll enjoy great views and pass through seven tunnels. Or, if you prefer a quicker paved route, take US 24 from Manitou Springs to Woodland Park and then pick up Colorado 67 south to Cripple Creek.

During the 1890s, Cripple Creek was the site of the last great gold rush in the United States. At the turn of the century, this mining district (including Goldfield and Victor) had a population of 100,000, making it the largest metropolitan area in Colorado. By the time of the Great Depression, Cripple Creek was practically abandoned, and the few remaining residents tore down the old empty houses for firewood. You can still see traces of old city streets extending for miles around the town that exists today. There is said to be more gold under Cripple Creek today than the total amount the mines produced during their heyday, but it would take more money than the mine would produce to replace the rusted equipment and tunnel support structures. In fact, few mines showed big profits even in the old days. Over 11,000 exploratory holes resulted in only 500 producing mines in the district, but many people made fortunes selling speculative stock in the other 10,500 tunnels (the Colorado Springs Mining Exchange, dealing only in Cripple Creek gold stocks, was once the second-largest stock exchange in America).

The best-known Cripple Creek gold tycoon was Winfield Scott Stratton, a carpenter from Colorado Springs who spent his summers prospecting. After five years of futile searching, he promised his wife that he would give up his quest, stay home, and earn a living for a change. But the lure of imagined gold proved too strong, and two years later he returned to Cripple Creek, where he dug down three feet in an abandoned claim and found the richest strike in the district. Lacking capital to mine it himself, Stratton sold the claim to an Eastern syndicate for $11 million and retired to become Colorado Springs' most prominent philanthropist. After expenses, the mine's new owners never recovered their capital investment.

Cripple Creek has one of the best mine tours in the Rockies. The **Molly Kathleen Mine** on Colorado 67 at the north end of town gives you a look at one of the veins that provided a portion of the $600 million worth of gold produced by this rich district. It's open from 9:00 a.m. to 5:00 p.m. May to October. Adults $7, children $3.50. (719) 689-2465. My favorite excursion in this area is the **Cripple Creek and Victor Narrow Gauge Railroad**, leading over to the sister city of Victor. Open 10:00 a.m. to 5:00 p.m. May to October. Adults $6, seniors $5.50, children $3. (719) 689-2640. Also of special interest are the **Cripple Creek Museum**, the **Imperial Melodrama Theater**, and the **Victor-Lowell Thomas Museum**, dedicated to the famous journalist and world traveler. He was born in this house and began his newspaper career in Victor. Like Central City and Black Hawk, Cripple Creek now has legalized gambling for limited stakes. The Gold

Camp Road and US 24/Colorado 67 both began as narrow gauge rail routes that carried supplies up to Cripple Creek and gold ore back down. A third narrow gauge railroad was built between Cripple Creek and Cañon City, but the train derailed on a trestle during its maiden trip and the railroad was never used thereafter. The rugged route is now the scenic unpaved road through Phantom Canyon (allow 3 hours for the trip). There is no paved road route between Cripple Creek and Cañon City. If you do want a paved route, you must return to Colorado Springs and take Colorado 115 and US 50 to Cañon City.

The most popular destination in Cañon City is the **Royal Gorge Suspension Bridge** spanning the chasm 1,053 feet above the Arkansas River. It is owned by the municipal government of Cañon City and generates enough tourist dollars to account for the majority of the town's operating budget. You can drive or walk across the rattly suspension bridge. You can also cross the gorge by aerial tramway or ride the inclined railway down the cliff to the river. Entrance plus your choice of two other attractions (tramway, incline, or theater) costs $8.50 for adults, $6.50 for children 4 to 11. (719) 275-7507. Here's something to ponder: when the tramway was built, they carried the cable across the gorge by helicopter. But in the 1920s when the suspension bridge was built, helicopters had not been invented yet. The bridge could not be started until the cables were already in place; and each cable weighs many tons. So how did they get the bridge cables from one side of the chasm to the other. Stumped? Ask an employee; they all know the story. You can stay overnight here or return to Colorado Springs via US 50 east and Colorado 115 north. The two dirt roads, Gold Camp and Phantom Canyon, are narrow and not recommended for trailers or RVs. Both roads should be driven with extreme care and avoided in inclement weather.

Third Day: Colorado Springs

On your last day in Colorado Springs you can choose from a variety of intriguing possibilities. **The U.S. Air Force Academy**, located at the north end of town off

I-25 (exit 150B or 156B) is open daily from 9:00 a.m. to 5:00 p.m. Self-guided tour maps are available at the Visitor Center, and there are afternoon planetarium programs Thursday through Sunday in the summer and on Sundays the rest of the year. (303) 472-2555. **The Western Museum of Mining and Industry** is located on North Gate Road on the east side of I-25, a short distance from the Air Force Academy. It's open from 9:00 a.m. to 4:00 p.m. (719) 598-8850. Returning south on I-25, take exit 147, Rockrimmon Boulevard West, to 101 Pro Rodeo Drive and turn left to the Pro Rodeo Hall of Fame, which operates jointly with the **Museum of the American Cowboy**. They are open in summer from 9:00 a.m. to 5:00 p.m. and the rest of the year from 9:00 a.m. to 4:30 p.m. (719) 593-8847.

Downtown at 423 N. Cascade Avenue is the historic **McAllister House**, the brick home of a Colorado Springs pioneer, where guided tours give you a look at handcrafted nineteenth-century furnishings. It's open May to August from 10:00 a.m. to 4:00 p.m. Wednesday through Saturday and noon to 4:00 p.m. on Sunday. (719) 635-7925. The rest of the year it's open Thursday through Saturday 10:00 a.m to 4:00 p.m. Also downtown is the **Colorado Springs Pioneers Museum**, 215 South Teton Street, which features exhibits on subjects ranging from quilting to Native American pottery. It's open Monday through Saturday 10:00 a.m. to 5:00 p.m. and Sunday 1:00 p.m. to 5:00 p.m. (719) 578-6650.

One of the hottest tours in Colorado Springs is the **North American Air Defense Command**. Advance reservations, made by calling (719) 554-7895, are a must for this tour, operated only on Saturdays. Call 6 months ahead to reserve your visit to this nuclear defense nerve center (which once detected an incoming missile that turned out to be the moon). The NORAD office will provide precise instructions on reaching the command post.

INDEX

Other Books from John Muir Publications

Adventure Vacations: From Trekking in New Guinea to Swimming in Siberia, Bangs 256 pp. $17.95

Asia Through the Back Door, 3rd ed., Steves and Gottberg 326 pp. $15.95

Belize: A Natural Destination, Mahler, Wotkyns, Schafer 304 pp. $16.95

Bus Touring: Charter Vacations, U.S.A., Warren with Bloch 168 pp. $9.95

California Public Gardens: A Visitor's Guide, Sigg 304 pp. $16.95

Catholic America: Self-Renewal Centers and Retreats, Christian-Meyer 325 pp. $13.95

Costa Rica: A Natural Destination, 2nd ed., Sheck 288 pp. $16.95

Elderhostels: The Students' Choice, 2nd ed., Hyman 312 pp. $15.95

Environmental Vacations: Volunteer Projects to Save the Planet, 2nd ed., Ocko 248 pp. $16.95

Europe 101: History & Art for the Traveler, 4th ed., Steves and Openshaw 372 pp. $15.95

Europe Through the Back Door, 10th ed., Steves 448 pp. $16.95

A Foreign Visitor's Guide to America, Baldwin and Levine 200 pp. $10.95 (avail. 9/92)

Floating Vacations: River, Lake, and Ocean Adventures, White 256 pp. $17.95

Great Cities of Eastern Europe, Rapoport 256 pp. $16.95

Gypsying After 40: A Guide to Adventure and Self-Discovery, Harris 264 pp. $14.95

The Heart of Jerusalem, Nellhaus 336 pp. $12.95

Indian America: A Traveler's Companion, 2nd ed., Eagle/Walking Turtle 448 pp. $17.95

Interior Furnishings Southwest: The Sourcebook of the Best Production Craftspeople, Deats and Villani 256 pp. $19.95 (avail. 9/92)

Mona Winks: Self-Guided Tours of Europe's Top Museums, Steves and Openshaw 456 pp. $14.95

Opera! The Guide to Western Europe's Great Houses, Zietz 296 pp. $18.95

Paintbrushes and Pistols: How the Taos Artists Sold the West, Taggett and Schwarz 280 pp. $17.95

The People's Guide to Mexico, 8th ed., Franz 608 pp. $17.95

The People's Guide to RV Camping in Mexico, Franz with Rogers 320 pp. $13.95

Ranch Vacations: The Complete Guide to Guest and Resort, Fly-Fishing, and Cross-Country Skiing Ranches, 2nd ed., Kilgore 396 pp. $18.95

The Shopper's Guide to Art and Crafts in the Hawaiian Islands, Schuchter 272 pp. $13.95

The Shopper's Guide to Mexico, Rogers and Rosa 224 pp. $9.95

Ski Tech's Guide to Equipment, Skiwear, and Accessories, ed. Tanler 144 pp. $11.95

Ski Tech's Guide to Maintenance and Repair, ed. Tanler 160 pp. $11.95

A Traveler's Guide to Asian Culture, Chambers 224 pp. $13.95

Traveler's Guide to Healing Centers and Retreats in North America, Rudee and Blease 240 pp. $11.95

Understanding Europeans, Miller 272 pp. $14.95

Undiscovered Islands of the Caribbean, 2nd ed., Willes 232 pp. $14.95

Undiscovered Islands of the Mediterranean, 2nd ed., Moyer and Willes 256 pp. $13.95

Undiscovered Islands of the U.S. and Canadian West Coast, Moyer and Willes 208 pp. $12.95

A Viewer's Guide to Art: A Glossary of Gods, People, and Creatures, Shaw and Warren 144 pp. $10.95

2 to 22 Days Series

Each title offers 22 flexible daily itineraries that can be used to get the most out of vacations of any length. Included are not only "must see" attractions but also little-known villages and hidden "jewels" as well as valuable general information.

22 Days Around the World, 1992 ed., Rapoport and Willes 256 pp. $12.95 **(1993 ed.** avail. 8/92)

2 to 22 Days Around the Great Lakes, 1992 ed., Schuchter 192 pp. $9.95

22 Days in Alaska, Lanier 128 pp. $7.95

2 to 22 Days in the American Southwest, 1992 ed., Harris 176 pp. $9.95

2 to 22 Days in Asia, 1992 ed., Rapoport and Willes 176 pp. $9.95 **(1993 ed.** avail. 8/92)

2 to 22 Days in Australia, 1992 ed., Gottberg 192 pp. $9.95 **(1993 ed.** avail. 8/92)

2 to 22 Days in California, 1992 ed., Rapoport 192 pp. $9.95 **(1993 ed.** avail. 8/92)

22 Days in China, Duke and Victor 144 pp. $7.95

2 to 22 Days in Europe, 1992 ed., Steves 276 pp. $12.95

2 to 22 Days in Florida, 1992 ed., Harris 192 pp. $9.95 **(1993 ed.** avail. 8/92)

2 to 22 Days in France, 1992 ed., Steves 192 pp. $9.95

2 to 22 Days in Germany, Austria, & Switzerland, 1992 ed., Steves 224 pp. $9.95

2 to 22 Days in Great Britain, 1992 ed., Steves 192 pp. $9.95

2 to 22 Days in Hawaii, 1992 ed., Schuchter 176 pp. $9.95 **(1993 ed.** avail. 8/92)

22 Days in India, Mathur 136 pp. $7.95

22 Days in Japan, Old 136 pp. $7.95

22 Days in Mexico, 2nd ed., Rogers and Rosa 128 pp. $7.95

2 to 22 Days in New England, 1992 ed., Wright 192 pp. $9.95

2 to 22 Days in New Zealand, 1992 ed., Schuchter 176 pp. $9.95 **(1993 ed.** avail. 8/92)

2 to 22 Days in Norway, Sweden, & Denmark, 1992 ed., Steves 192 pp. $9.95

2 to 22 Days in the Pacific Northwest, 1992 ed., Harris 192 pp. $9.95

2 to 22 Days in the Rockies, 1992 ed., Rapoport 176 pp. $9.95

2 to 22 Days in Spain & Portugal, 1992 ed., Steves 192 pp. $9.95

2 to 22 Days in Texas, 1992 ed., Harris 192 pp. $9.95 **(1993 ed.** avail. 8/92)

2 to 22 Days in Thailand, 1992 ed., Richardson 176 pp. $9.95
(1993 ed. avail. 8/92)
22 Days in the West Indies, Morreale and Morreale 136 pp. $7.95

Parenting Series
Being a Father: Family, Work, and Self, *Mothering* Magazine
176 pp. $12.95
**Preconception: A Woman's Guide to Preparing for Pregnancy
and Parenthood,** Aikey-Keller 232 pp. $14.95
Schooling at Home: Parents, Kids, and Learning, *Mothering*
Magazine 264 pp. $14.95
Teens: A Fresh Look, *Mothering* Magazine 240 pp. $14.95

"Kidding Around" Travel Guides for Young Readers
Written for kids eight years of age and older.
Kidding Around Atlanta, Pedersen 64 pp. $9.95
Kidding Around Boston, Byers 64 pp. $9.95
Kidding Around Chicago, Davis 64 pp. $9.95
Kidding Around the Hawaiian Islands, Lovett 64 pp. $9.95
Kidding Around London, Lovett 64 pp. $9.95
Kidding Around Los Angeles, Cash 64 pp. $9.95
Kidding Around the National Parks of the Southwest, Lovett
108 pp. $12.95
Kidding Around New York City, Lovett 64 pp. $9.95
Kidding Around Paris, Clay 64 pp. $9.95
Kidding Around Philadelphia, Clay 64 pp. $9.95
Kidding Around San Diego, Luhrs 64 pp. $9.95
Kidding Around San Francisco, Zibart 64 pp. $9.95
Kidding Around Santa Fe, York 64 pp. $9.95
Kidding Around Seattle, Steves 64 pp. $9.95
Kidding Around Spain, Biggs 108 pp. $12.95
Kidding Around Washington, D.C., Pedersen 64 pp. $9.95

"Extremely Weird" Series for Young Readers
Written for kids eight years of age and older.
Extremely Weird Bats, Lovett 48 pp. $9.95
Extremely Weird Birds, Lovett 48 pp. $9.95
Extremely Weird Endangered Species, Lovett 48 pp. $9.95
Extremely Weird Fishes, Lovett 48 pp. $9.95
Extremely Weird Frogs, Lovett 48 pp. $9.95
Extremely Weird Primates, Lovett 48 pp. $9.95
Extremely Weird Reptiles, Lovett 48 pp. $9.95
Extremely Weird Spiders, Lovett 48 pp. $9.95

Masters of Motion Series
For kids eight years and older.
How to Drive an Indy Race Car, Rubel 48 pages $9.95 paper
(avail. 8/92)
How to Fly a 747, Paulson 48 pages $9.95 (avail. 9/92)
How to Fly the Space Shuttle, Shorto 48 pages $9.95 paper
(avail. 10/92)

Quill Hedgehog Adventures Series
Green fiction for kids. Written for kids eight years of age and older.
Quill's Adventures in the Great Beyond. Waddington-Feather
96 pp. $5.95
Quill's Adventures in Wasteland, Waddington-Feather 132 pp. $5.95
Quill's Adventures in Grozzieland, Waddington-Feather 132 pp. $5.95

X-ray Vision Series
For kids eight years and older.

Looking Inside Cartoon Animation, Schultz 48 pages $9.95 paper
(avail. 9/92)
Looking Inside Sports Aerodynamics, Schultz 48 pages $9.95
paper (avail. 9/92)
Looking Inside the Brain, Schultz 48 pages $9.95 paper

Other Young Readers Titles

The Indian Way: Learning to Communicate with Mother Earth,
McLain 114 pp. $9.95
The Kids' Environment Book: What's Awry and Why, Pedersen
192 pp. $13.95
Kids Explore America's Hispanic Heritage, Westridge Young
Writers Workshop 112 pp. $7.95
**Rads, Ergs, and Cheeseburgers: The Kids' Guide to Energy and
the Environment,** Yanda 108 pp. $12.95

Automotive Titles

How to Keep Your VW Alive, 14th ed., 440 pp. $21.95
How to Keep Your Subaru Alive 480 pp. $21.95
How to Keep Your Toyota Pickup Alive 392 pp. $21.95
How to Keep Your Datsun/Nissan Alive 544 pp. $21.95
**The Greaseless Guide to Car Care Confidence: Take the Terror
Out of Talking to Your Mechanic,** Jackson 224 pp. $14.95
Off-Road Emergency Repair & Survival, Ristow 160 pp. $9.95

Ordering Information
If you cannot find our books in your local bookstore, you can order
directly from us. Please check the "Available" date above. If you
send us money for a book not yet available, we will hold your money
until we can ship you the book. Your books will be sent to you via
UPS (for U.S. destinations). UPS will not deliver to a P.O. Box;
please give us a street address. Include $3.75 for the first item
ordered and $.50 for each additional item to cover shipping and
handling costs. For airmail within the U.S., enclose $4.00. All foreign
orders will be shipped surface rate; please enclose $3.00 for the
first item and $1.00 for each additional item. Please inquire about
foreign airmail rates.

Method of Payment
Your order may be paid by check, money order, or credit card. We
cannot be responsible for cash sent through the mail. All payments
must be made in U.S. dollars drawn on a U.S. bank. Canadian
postal money orders in U.S. dollars are acceptable. For VISA,
MasterCard, or American Express orders, include your card number, expiration date, and your signature, or call (800) 888-7504.
Books ordered on American Express cards can be shipped only to
the billing address of the cardholder. Sorry, no C.O.D.'s. Residents
of sunny New Mexico, add 5.875% tax to the total.

Address all orders and inquiries to:
John Muir Publications
P.O. Box 613
Santa Fe, NM 87504
(505) 982-4078
(800) 888-7504